For Linda - I hope you enjoy reading this as much as I enjoyed writing it - Bruce

Tom, Scott & Zelda

Following In Their Footsteps

Bruce E. Johnson

Thomas Wolfe Memorial
Literary Award Recipient

B—— 2020

Copyright © 2019 by Bruce E. Johnson.
Second Edition May 2019

All rights reserved. No part of this book may be reproduced in any form or by any electronic or mechanical means, including information storage and retrieval systems, without permission in writing from the publisher, except by a reviewer, who may quote brief passages in a review.

Published by Knock On Wood Publications
A Division of Wood-Care, Inc.
Asheville, N.C.

ISBN 978-1-5323-9818-6

Quotations from *Look Homeward, Angel*
courtesy of Charles Scribner's Sons
New York, N.Y.

Cover design by William Murphy.

Cover Photos, Front:

Scott and Zelda Fitzgerald courtesy of and © by the Princeton University Library.

Thomas Wolfe in Asheville cabin from the Thomas Wolfe Collection,
Pack Memorial Library, Asheville, N.C.

Cover Photos, Back:

Old Kentucky Home at the Thomas Wolfe Memorial State Historic Site.

Front Entrance, Grove Park Inn, Asheville.

Tom, Scott & Zelda

Following In Their Footsteps

I think no one could understand Thomas Wolfe
who had not seen or properly imagined
the place in which he was born
and grew up.

~ Maxwell Perkins, editor

Books by Bruce E. Johnson

Grant Wood: The 19 Lithographs
The Dark Side of Paradise
Tales of the Grove Park Inn
Arts and Crafts Shopmarks
An Unexpected Guest
The Grove Park Inn's Arts & Crafts Collection
The Artistry of William Waldo Dodge, Jr.
Built for the Ages: A History of the Grove Park Inn
The Official Identification and Price Guide
To the Arts & Crafts Movement: 1895-1923
50 Simple Ways To Save Your House
The Pegged Joint
The Wood Finisher
The Weekend Refinisher
Craftsman Furniture by Gustav Stickley (edited)
Dedham Pottery Catalog (edited)
How To Make $20,000 A Year In Antiques –
Without Leaving Your Job
Knock On Wood
Inherit the Wind & The Scopes Monkey Trial: A Study Guide
Kidnapped: A Study Guide

www.BruceJohnsonBooks.com

Table of Contents

About This Book

As a former literature teacher, arriving in Asheville and discovering that Thomas Wolfe had grown up in this mountain oasis and F. Scott Fitzgerald had lived for nearly two years in the Grove Park Inn was almost beyond comprehension. All I needed was for Ernest Hemingway to have bought William Faulkner a couple of mint juleps in the rooftop bar of the George Vanderbilt Hotel and I would have been in literary heaven.

But having two twentieth-century literary icons living in one small Southern city was certainly enough material for one intoxicating study, especially given that all four of these writers had legendary drinking habits. Fitzgerald could down a dozen bottles of beer in a day. Wolfe preferred his whiskey straight up. Hemingway loved to linger over a chilled martini and Faulkner savored his afternoon mint juleps, once declaring, "Pouring out liquor is like burning books." Still open to debate is whether their creative muses relied on their favorite drinks, or whether Scott Fitzgerald was right: "First, you take a drink, then the drink takes a drink, then the drink takes you."

Eventually, then, I took some sage advice from yet another author: "Write the book you always wanted to read."

This book can be used in two different ways. First, it can serve as a walking and driving guide as you literally follow in the footsteps of Thomas Wolfe, Zelda Fitzgerald, and F. Scott Fitzgerald. In addition, it can also be enjoyed in a comfortable chair, as you learn more about their three entwined lives. Either way, it is written so that you can read any selection in any order without having to read it from cover to cover.

Tom Wolfe declared that "a novelist might turn over half the characters in his native town to make a single figure." Likewise, an historian might turn over nearly every book ever written about his subject to make a single book. I was fortunate to have been able to draw upon the research and publications of several biographers and area historians without whom this book could never have been completed. Among them were Richard Hansley, Joshua Darty, Jack Thomson, Matthew Bruccoli, Andrew Turnbull, LeGette Blythe, Elizabeth Nowell, Tony Buttitta, John C. Griffin, Jeffrey Neyers, Hayden Norwood, David Herbert Donald, Joanne Marshall Maudlin, Ted Mitchell, Floyd Watkins, Constance Richards, Wilma Dykeman, Nancy Milford, John S. Phillipson, Douglas Stewart McDaniel, Bob

Terrell, Rob Neufeld, George W. McCoy, Jennifer Prince, Myra Champion, Lou Harshaw, and the fabulous staff at the Thomas Wolfe Memorial State Historic Site who watch over the Old Kentucky Home.

Historic photographs for this book were generously supplied by the dedicated research staff in the North Carolina Room of Pack Memorial Library, including Zoe Rhine, Ione Whitlock, and Katherine Calhoun Cutshall; by Mark Burdette at the Hendersonville County Public Library; and by Patrick Bryant at the Lake Lure Inn. My good friend Bill Murphy worked tirelessly to sharpen and re-size every photograph; without his personal and professional attention to detail, they could not have become one of this book's most effective tools.

Even after multiple drafts, my near-final manuscript still had rough edges which needed to be smoothed out. Fortunately, Kieta Osteen-Cochrane, a member of the board for the Preservation Society of Asheville and Buncombe County, carefully culled through my text, correcting my numerous inconsistencies.

And from the very beginning of this project, I was always assisted and encouraged by my patient editorial assistant Kate Nixon; by my dear friends Jim Wilson and Lynne Poirier-Wilson; and by my remarkable and always supportive wife Leigh Ann.

Finally, I wish to dedicate this book to my talented and tireless mother, Marcia Hickok Johnson, who passed away on August 14, 2018, after eighty-eight years of being a devoted daughter, wife, mother, and teacher. She instilled in me a love for both reading and research, and sharing all which you discover with those who share your passion.

– Bruce E. Johnson

Western North Carolina

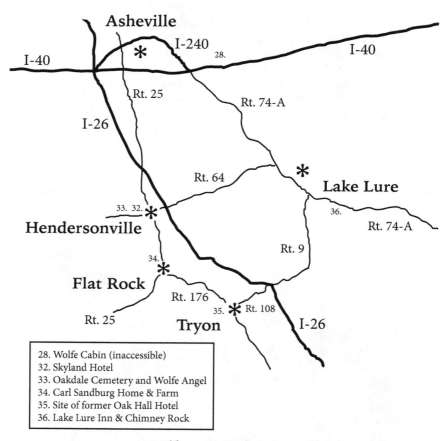

Asheville

I-40

I-240

28.

I-40

Rt. 25

Rt. 74-A

I-26

Rt. 64

Lake Lure

33. 32.

Hendersonville

36.

Rt. 74-A

34.

Rt. 9

Flat Rock

Rt. 176

Rt. 25

35. Rt. 108

Tryon

I-26

28. Wolfe Cabin (inaccessible)
32. Skyland Hotel
33. Oakdale Cemetery and Wolfe Angel
34. Carl Sandburg Home & Farm
35. Site of former Oak Hall Hotel
36. Lake Lure Inn & Chimney Rock

Miles & Minutes

Asheville to Hendersonville	26 miles	33 minutes
Hendersonville to Tryon	23 miles	29 minutes
Tryon to Lake Lure	19 miles	31 minutes
Lake Lure to Asheville	28 miles	48 minutes
Asheville to Tryon	45 miles	51 minutes
Hendersonville to Lake Lure	20 miles	36 minutes

Asheville

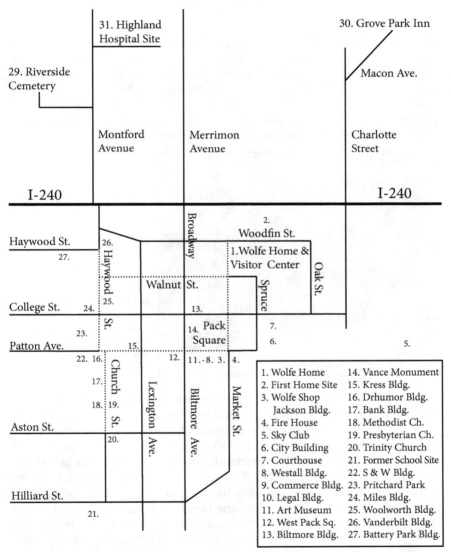

31. Highland Hospital Site

30. Grove Park Inn

29. Riverside Cemetery

Macon Ave.

Montford Avenue

Merrimon Avenue

Charlotte Street

I-240

I-240

Haywood St.

26.

27.

Broadway

2.
Woodfin St.

1.Wolfe Home & Visitor Center

Oak St.

Haywood St.

Walnut St.

Spruce

College St.

24.

25.

13.

23.

14. Pack Square

7.

Patton Ave.

15.

6.

5.

22. 16.

Church St.

12.

11.-8. 3.

4.

17.

Lexington Ave.

Biltmore Ave.

Market St.

18.

19.

Aston St.

20.

Hilliard St.

21.

1. Wolfe Home	14. Vance Monument
2. First Home Site	15. Kress Bldg.
3. Wolfe Shop Jackson Bldg.	16. Drhumor Bldg.
	17. Bank Bldg.
4. Fire House	18. Methodist Ch.
5. Sky Club	19. Presbyterian Ch.
6. City Building	20. Trinity Church
7. Courthouse	21. Former School Site
8. Westall Bldg.	22. S & W Bldg.
9. Commerce Bldg.	23. Pritchard Park
10. Legal Bldg.	24. Miles Bldg.
11. Art Museum	25. Woolworth Bldg.
12. West Pack Sq.	26. Vanderbilt Bldg.
13. Biltmore Bldg.	27. Battery Park Bldg.

Please Note: For simplification, these maps are not drawn to scale and several streets and roads have been omitted. Site locations are approximate. Please consult a more detailed map for specific directions. Dotted line is suggested route.

11.

Thomas Clayton Wolfe
1900 - 1938

Thomas Clayton Wolfe was born on October 3, 1900, at his family's home at 48 Spruce Street in Asheville. He was the seventh surviving child of the stormy marriage between Julia Westall Wolfe and William Oliver Wolfe. In 1906 Julia Wolfe purchased the Old Kentucky Home, a boarding house at 48 Spruce Street, just two blocks from the Wolfe family home. She and six-year-old Tom moved into the boarding house, which could sleep as many as nineteen boarders.

Julia Wolfe's Old Kentucky Home with W.O. Wolfe to the left and Tom to the right. (Thomas Wolfe Collection, Pack Memorial Library, Asheville, NC)

While Julia ran the boarding house, W.O. Wolfe, a chronic alcoholic, operated a tombstone shop a few blocks away on Pack Square. Tom and the other Wolfe children roamed between the two houses and the shop, depending on where they were most needed: tending to their mother's boarders or to their demanding father. A few weeks before his sixth birthday, Tom enrolled in the nearby Orange Street School, where he completed his first eight grades. Rather than enter public high school, Tom convinced his parents to pay one hundred dollars for him to attend the private North State Fitting School. Margaret Roberts, his teacher, took Tom under her maternal wing, encouraging him to develop his writing ability and to expand the scope of his reading. Although he called her "the mother of my spirit," neither she nor her husband John, like nearly 300 other townspeople, escaped unscathed in *Look Homeward, Angel.*

In 1916, Tom enrolled in the University of North Carolina at Chapel Hill, where he soon overcame the typical freshman insecurities, rising to become one of the most popular upperclassmen on campus. He directed his creative energy into writing, later enrolling in the Master of Fine Arts program at Harvard, but his attempts at playwriting proved too long and too verbose to attract the sustained interest of any producers. He earned his Master's Degree from Harvard but was unable to convince any theatre companies to stage his lengthy plays. To survive, Wolfe accepted a position as an English instructor at New York University, where he taught from 1924 until 1930.

Tom took time in 1924 to make his first trip to Europe. On the voyage home he met Aline Bernstein, a married costume and set designer nearly twenty years older than Tom. Bernstein, in addition to recognizing his streak of unbridled genius, fell in love with the frustrated writer. Providing both financial and emotional support, Aline Bernstein encouraged her young lover to forgo playwriting, turning his attention instead to writing his first novel. Edited by Maxwell Perkins and published by Charles Scribner's Sons in 1929, Thomas Wolfe dedicated *Look Homeward, Angel* to her.

While the novel garnered positive, if restrained reviews in the literary world, it was met with shock and anger in Asheville. It was not, as one resident declared, that they denied their scandals, flaws, and bad behavior, but that Wolfe had chosen to expose them to the entire world with their actual names so thinly disguised that no one questioned who was being lampooned, including his father, mother, brothers, and sisters. The outcry was so vociferous that for the next eight years, Tom Wolfe feared he couldn't go home again.

The success of *Look Homeward, Angel* soon enabled Wolfe to resign his teaching position, return to Europe several times, and live in New York City, where in 1935 he completed his second novel, *Of Time and the River*, as well as a collection of short stories entitled *From Death to Morning*. His personal life fell into shambles, however, as his relationship with Aline Bernstein soured into an embarrassing and expensive distraction. He also proved unable to manage his finances or to write on a regular schedule. Like his father and older brother Frank, he too often turned to alcohol, and often ruined dinner parties, ruptured friendships, and strained his relationship with Maxwell Perkins and the Scribner's staff to the breaking point. As one astute reviewer remarked in a well-publicized magazine article, "Genius is not enough."

In 1937 his family and friends convinced Tom that the people of Asheville now recognized their prodigal author as a national celebrity and had forgiven, though not forgotten, how he had portrayed them in his novels. That May he spent two weeks in the Old Kentucky Home boarding house (right, with mother), then returned to New York. There he organized his manuscripts in preparation for an extended stay at a friend's secluded cabin outside Asheville. If Wolfe had hoped to replicate Thoreau's time at Walden Pond at an Asheville cabin overlooking the Swannanoa River, he was soon disappointed, as a steady stream of well-wishers, autograph seekers, and revelers disrupted his daily writing schedule.

Tom and mother Julia, 1937.
(Thomas Wolfe Collection, Pack
Memorial Library, Asheville, NC)

In the summer of 1938, Tom embarked on a trip to the West Coast, where in July he contracted a severe cold which quickly developed into pneumonia. His severe coughing ruptured a dormant tuberculosis lesion in his right lung, sending tubercular cells through his bloodstream and into his brain tissue, where they fanned out like a fatal spider web. Exploratory surgery at Johns Hopkins Hospital revealed his condition to be terminal. Tom died three days later on September 15, 1938. His funeral was held in the First Presbyterian Church he had attended as a child, and burial took place afterwards in Asheville's Riverside Cemetery.

After Tom's death, Edward Aswell, his new editor at Harper and Brother's, labored for months over the large pile of raw bundles of handwritten manuscripts left behind. Totaling more than one million words, Tom had only begun to organize them into chapters for his next two novels. Though admittedly far from perfect, Aswell released two posthumous novels: *The Web and the Rock* (1939) and *You Can't Go Home Again* (1940), as well as another collection of short stories, *The Hills Beyond* (1941).

As an assessment of his brief literary life, a writer for the *New York Times* concluded, "His was one of the most confident young voices in contemporary American literature, a vibrant, full-toned voice which it is hard to believe could be so suddenly stilled. The stamp of genius was upon him, though it was an undisciplined and unpredictable genius. There was within him an unspent energy, an untiring force, an unappeasable hunger for life and for expression which might have carried him to the heights — and might equally have torn him down."

F. Scott Fitzgerald
1896 - 1940

Zelda Sayre Fitzgerald
1900 - 1948

Born four years and two worlds apart, in 1918 private Francis Scott Fitzgerald met Zelda Sayre, the belle of Montgomery, Alabama, at a dance near Fort Sheridan, where he was stationed. Born in 1896, Scott had grown up in St. Paul, Minnesota, where his father struggled to provide for his family. In contrast, Zelda's father was a respected judge, providing her with ample opportunity to entertain and socialize in Montgomery. A free spirit, Zelda enjoyed being courted by the young men in town, as well as by the Fort Sheridan soldiers. While Scott was immediately smitten by her vivacious personality and infamous beauty, Zelda didn't feel the Princeton dropout spouting dreams of becoming a successful novelist met her criteria for a future husband. "I was in love with a dazzling light," Scott wrote. "I thought she was a goddess."

Scott, "Scottie," and Zelda.   *(Photo courtesy and © Princeton University Library.)*

Determined to change her mind, Scott returned to St. Paul where he completed the manuscript for *This Side of Paradise*. Once released by Scribner's in 1920, it skyrocketed up the best seller lists, prompting nineteen-year-old Zelda to marry Scott in New York City on April 3. For the next decade the young couple played the role of the ultimate Roaring Twenties couple, traveling across Europe, staying in the Plaza Hotel in New York, drinking at the Ritz Bar in Paris, vacationing on the Riviera, and showing up at parties at midnight and staying until dawn. "Going at top speed," Scott recalled, "in the gayest worlds we could find."

On the surface their next five years seemed like a fairy tale romance, as Scott became the highest paid short story writer in America, earning as much as $3,000 per story. They vacationed across Europe, and in October of 1921 Zelda gave birth to Scottie, their only child. The next year Scott published another successful novel, as well as a popular collection of short stories. All the while, however, Scott and Zelda were silently drowning in debt and slowly destroying each other's self-confidence.

In 1925 their troubles began to surface. *The Great Gatsby* was a critical success, but sales were disappointing. A bored Zelda had a fling with a French aviator, which sent Scott into a jealous rage and ignited an intense resentment which he harbored for years. Unable to control their spending, the couple became mired in debt, both financially and emotionally. A distraught Zelda took up writing and ballet, neither of which she was able to master, while Scott turned into an alcoholic in search of his lost capacity to write.

In 1930 Zelda suffered the first of several nervous breakdowns and was hospitalized in a Swiss sanitarium, where the doctors diagnosed her as schizophrenic. The next year Scott and Zelda returned to the

Zelda and Scott. (Photo courtesy and © by Princeton University Library.)

states, where Scott took a screenwriting job to pay for Zelda's treatment at Johns Hopkins University Hospital in Baltimore, as well as their daughter's private schooling in Connecticut and his own wasteful lifestyle. In 1932, while he struggled to complete a sequel to *The Great Gatsby*, Scribner's published Zelda's autobiographical novel *Save Me the Waltz*. It was a total failure, and Scott's 1934 *Tender Is the Night* did not fare well enough to pull them out of debt. Zelda fell deeper into despair, while Scott fell deeper into drink.

Hoping to revitalize his writing career, in 1935 Scott withdrew to North Carolina. During the next two years he careened between a series of hotels, including the Grove Park Inn, the Oak Hall Hotel, the Skyland Hotel, the Battery Park Hotel, and the Lake Lure Inn, still searching for his lost inspiration. Convinced he had tuberculosis, Scott used his poor health as an excuse for his failure to regain his status as America's most popular short story writer. In truth, it was brought on by his incessant smoking, drinking, and poor eating habits. With Zelda still in Baltimore, Scott literally fell into the arms of a young, married admirer who was also staying at the Grove Park Inn. Their disastrous affair further complicated his life and paralyzed his writing skills that summer.

After ending his affair, Scott brought Zelda to Asheville in April of 1936, turning her over to the care of Dr. Carroll and the staff at Highland Hospital. On an outing together, Scott dislocated his shoulder and broke his collarbone attempting a high dive at a local swimming pool. Encased in an upper body cast for six weeks, Scott became even more despondent, depending on both beer and gin to be able to dictate what turned out to be his most mediocre work. That September a reporter for the *New York Post* interviewed Scott in his room at the Grove Park Inn for an article entitled "The Other Side of Paradise, Scott Fitzgerald, 40, Engulfed in Despair." Upon reading what amounted to his literary obituary, Scott attempted suicide by swallowing a bottle of pain pills, but vomited on the bathroom floor before they could take effect.

Sensing he had outstayed his welcome at the Grove Park Inn, Scott returned to the Oak Hall Hotel in Tryon, where he stayed for the first six months of 1937. That July he accepted a desperately needed offer to return to Hollywood as a screenwriter. After two frustrating years, however, M-G-M refused to renew his contract. On December 21, 1940, while living with gossip columnist Sheila Graham, the 44-year-old Fitzgerald died of a heart attack while working on *The Last Tycoon*.

Still at Highland Hospital, Zelda showed slow but steady improvement. The same year as Scott's death she was released to the care of her mother in Montgomery. In 1943 Scottie was married in New York, but Zelda was not well enough to attend. When she felt it necessary, Zelda checked herself back into Highland Hospital for additional, albeit questionable, treatments. On one return visit, on March 10, 1948, Zelda and eight other patients died in a fire originating in the basement of the old wooden building. She was just forty-eight. Zelda is buried alongside Scott in Rockville, Maryland.

The Thomas Wolfe Memorial State Historic Site

1. The Visitor Center

Information: Located at 52 North Market Street, the Thomas Wolfe Memorial Visitor Center is open Tuesday through Saturday from 9:00am until 5:00pm. The Visitor Center and the Old Kentucky Home are closed each Sunday and Monday, as well as on North Carolina state holidays.

House tours take place each day at half past each hour, with the final tour at 4:30pm. Group tours require advance reservations. Entrance fees are subject to change, but currently are five dollars for adults; two dollars for students ages seven through seventeen; and no charge for children six and younger. For additional information, including tours of Riverside Cemetery and other special events, please go to WolfeMemorial.com or call (828) 253-8304.

Old Kentucky Home. *(Thomas Wolfe Collection, Pack Memorial Library, Asheville.)*

Julia Wolfe, mother of Thomas Wolfe, operated the Old Kentucky Home from 1906 until her death in 1945 at the age of 85. In 1939 Wachovia Bank initiated foreclosure proceedings in an attempt to recover loans they had made to Julia during the Great Depression. Learning of her plight, Asheville business-man Harry Bloomberg paid off the loans, but allowed Julia to continue to operate the boarding house. In 1942 Bloomberg sold the house back to the Wolfe family, partitioning off an adjacent parcel of land for his own use.

Realizing they could not continue to maintain the 66-year-old structure, in 1949 the Wolfe family sold the home for approximately $15,000 to the new non-profit Thomas Wolfe Memorial Association. The association's members worked closely with the Wolfe siblings to trans-form the house into a memorial for their brother, maintaining the original furnishings and recreating how the boarding house would have appeared during Tom's years there. It opened on July 19, 1949, and attracted more than 1,300 visitors the first year.

In 1958 the City of Asheville assumed responsibility for the home, which was deemed a National Historic Landmark in 1971. Two years later ownership was transferred to the State of North Carolina. The Thomas Wolfe Memorial is now managed by the Historic Sites Section of the North Carolina Office of Archives and History.

Dedication ceremonies for the Visitor Center took place on Octo-ber 5, 1997, during the Thomas Wolfe Festival. The dedication commem-orated the completion of the auditorium and exhibition hall. Less than one year later, an arsonist set fire to the Old Kentucky Home, destroy-ing the dining room and inflicting damage on every room in the house, in addition to consuming more than two hundred antique artifacts. The fire was so extensive that the home was closed for six years before the $2.4 million restoration could be completed. Despite the extensive dam-age, the staff continued to keep the Visitor Center open and offered tours around the exterior of the fire-ravaged house.

The Old Kentucky Home reopened in 2004 and today hosts more than 20,000 visitors annually. The experience begins in the Visitor Cen-ter, which has a comprehensive selection of books written by and about Thomas Wolfe in the lobby. Nearby is an in-depth display of historical photographs, quotations from his works, copies of first editions, and items from the various stages of Tom's life and that of his family. Includ-ed are several of the tools from W.O. Wolfe's tombstone shop on Pack Square, as well as his safe and desk, furniture from the original Wolfe family home, artifacts dug out of an old cistern beside the Old Kentucky Home, personal items from Tom's apartment and hotel room in New York, and his infamous brown suit which he wore nearly everywhere. In addition, the staff has created a twenty-two-minute video which serves as an introduction to the guided tour through the Old Kentucky Home, led by one of their experienced and enthusiastic volunteers.

The Playhouse

1900, moved in 1955 to 48 Spruce Street

The tour of Julia Wolfe's Old Kentucky Home begins in the back yard beside the wooden shed William O. Wolfe constructed around 1900 as a playhouse for their children. The playhouse, however, had actually originated at 92 Woodfin Street (shown below), the first Wolfe family home, where all of the children had been born. It was located just two blocks northeast of the Old Kentucky Home in what is now the parking lot for the YMCA. When the Wolfe family home was demolished in 1955, local residents saved the playhouse by moving it to the yard of the Old Kentucky Home, protected since 1949 by the Thomas Wolfe Memorial Association. Even the modest playhouse made an appearance in *Look Homeward, Angel*:

"The playhouse was another of the strange extravagancies of Gantian [W.O. Wolfe] fancy: it had been built for the children when they were young. It had been for many years closed, it was a retreat of delight; its imprisoned air, stale and cool, was scented permanently with old pine boards, and dusty magazines." – Look Homeward, Angel

Covered with white painted shiplap boards, the spacious one-room playhouse can be viewed through a glass door. Inside the staff has collected an assortment of period toys, a vintage couch, and a child's chalkboard. A wood-burning stove used to heat the playhouse sits along the rear wall. Like the exterior, W.O. had covered the interior walls and tall ceiling with pine boards.

Playhouse at its original site.
(Thomas Wolfe Collection, Pack Memorial Library, Asheville, NC.)

20.

The Old Kentucky Home

1883
48 Spruce Street

"Dixieland. It was situated five minutes from the public square, on a pleasant sloping middleclass street of small homes and boarding-houses. Dixieland was a big cheaply constructed frame house of eighteen or twenty drafty high-ceilinged rooms: it had a rambling, unplanned, gabular appearance, and was painted a dirty yellow. It had a pleasant green front yard, not deep but wide, bordered by a row of young deep-bodied maples." – Look Homeward, Angel

In August of 1906 Julia Wolfe placed a down payment on a sprawling boarding house located at 48 Spruce Street, just two blocks from the Wolfe family residence at 92 Woodfin Street.

Constructed by an Asheville banker in 1883, what began as a seven-room house had undergone a major renovation and expansion by 1889, when it was converted to a private boarding house. When the proprietor died in 1900, the house was purchased by a Kentucky couple, Reverend Thomas M. Myers and his wife Mary, who renamed it the Old Kentucky Home.

When the Myers decided to sell the property in 1906, Julia Wolfe purchased the boarding house, opting to maintain the name of the Old Kentucky Home to both honor the Myers and placate their regular boarders. There were nineteen at the time of the sale, each paying eight dollars a week in exchange for a bed, breakfast, and dinner each day.

Initially, W.O. Wolfe approved his wife's idea and co-signed the mortgage, as he feared his aging hands would soon be unable to hold the hammer and chisel all day long in his tombstone shop on the square. In August of 1906 Julia packed up six-year-old Thomas and moved into the boarding house, leaving W.O. and the other five remaining children to fend for themselves. Sixteen-year-old Mabel ran the Wolfe household.

Young Tom was allowed to wander between the two houses. Where he stayed often depended on how crowded it was in the boarding house. But his mother insisted that he spend each night with her, even though Tom had no room of his own, having to seek out whatever bed his mother had not leased for the night.

Julia Wolfe's stinginess enabled her to pay off the mortgage quickly, but it also affected the quality of the Old Kentucky Home. One of her own relatives described it as "an untidy, dirty, squalid, down at the heels, second-class board house. Drab as to furniture, meager in food."

In 1916 Julia Wolfe undertook another renovation to the house, adding three sleeping porches, enlarging the dining room, and squeezing in additional bedrooms and bathrooms wherever possible to maximize every square foot of available space. By the time she had finished, her 6,000-square-foot house boasted twenty-nine rooms.

"The construction was after her own plans, and of the cheapest material: it never lost the smell of raw wood, cheap varnish, and flimsy rough plastering, but she had added eight or ten rooms at a cost of only $3,000."
– Look Homeward, Angel

Sleeping Porch.   (Thomas Wolfe Collection, Pack Memorial Library)

There were some pleasant times for Tom and the Wolfe family at the Old Kentucky Home, where the two daughters, Effie and Mabel, both held their weddings. But the boarding house had caused a rift in the family, as W.O. Wolfe did not move out of the family home he had built until 1917, when the advance of his prostate cancer made it impossible for him to either work or live alone. He was living at Julia's boarding house in 1918 when their 26-year-old son Ben, his health most likely compromised by latent tuberculosis, died from pneumonia brought on by the flu epidemic. Four years later W.O. died there of prostate cancer.

Tom left the boarding house in the fall of 1916 to enroll in the University of North Carolina at Chapel Hill. Memories of life amid the strangers wandering about the Old Kentucky Home were seared in his memory, however, as years later he recalled when writing his autobiographical novel:

"Eugene was ashamed of Dixieland . . . . He hated the indecency of his life, the loss of dignity and seclusion, the surrender of the tumultuous rabble of the four walls which shielded us from them. He felt, rather than understood, the waste, the confusion, the blind cruelty of their lives. . . . There was no place sacred unto themselves, no place fixed for their own inhabitation, no place proof against the invasion of the boarders."

The Fitzgerald's
at the Old Kentucky Home

In June of 1935, F. Scott Fitzgerald, recuperating from exhaustion and battling alcoholism, was staying in rooms 441 and 443 at the Grove Park Inn, where he had begun an affair with Beatrice Dance, a married woman staying there for the summer with her invalid sister. The next month her sister, upon discovering the affair, wrote Beatrice's husband and insisted he come to Asheville to retrieve them both. Fearful of an encounter with a jealous husband, Scott began searching for new accommodations. An Asheville friend, well aware that Scott and Tom Wolfe knew each other, suggested Julia Wolfe's Old Kentucky Home.

"I warned him that the Old Kentucky Home was no place for someone living in his style. It was a rambling old house, rundown and dismal, but no worse than the Skyland in Hendersonville where he had taken a dollar room the previous winter."
– After the Good Gay Times

One July afternoon Scott and Tony Buttitta stepped onto the covered porch lined with empty rocking chairs and gently knocked on the screen door. They were met by Julia Wolfe, who, as she was accustomed to doing with tourists, began regaling them with stories of her famous son. Tom, living in New York, had just returned from Europe to celebrate the success of his second novel *Of Time and the River*. He still had not visited his hometown since the publication of *Look Homeward, Angel* six years earlier.

Neither Buttitta nor Scott let on who he was, and Mrs. Wolfe apparently did not recognize her son's contemporary. After a routine tour of the house, the trio returned to the front porch, where a pallid and shaky Scott, somewhat overwhelmed by Mrs. Wolfe and most likely in need of another shot of gin, leaned against a post for support. Suspicious, Mrs. Wolfe leaned forward, smelled his breath, and declared, "I never take drunks – not if I know it." At that she spun around and marched back into the house, slamming the door behind her.

At the car Scott turned and looked back at the house. "Poor Tom! Poor bastard! She's a worse peasant than my mother!"

Zelda Fitzgerald also made a visit to the Old Kentucky Home, but without Scott. In 1940, after four years of treatment at Highland Hospital for anxiety and schizophrenia, Zelda had improved to the point where she was released to the care of her mother in Montgomery. In the summer of 1943 Zelda returned to Asheville for additional treatment.

While there she wrote a friend, "Asheville is haunted by unhappy, uncharted remembrance for me."

On September 6, 1943, perhaps seeking fresh living quarters un-inhabited by ghosts from her past, Zelda signed the guest register at the Old Kentucky Home, following Julia Wolfe up the stairs to a second-floor room "with two windows for $3.50 a week."

Records at the boarding house do not indicate how long Zelda stayed at the downtown boarding house, but one biographer believes that Zelda and Julia Wolfe became good friends. While the two women might very well have shared their experiences with famous authors who died tragically young, no documentation has surfaced to indicate Zelda stayed at the boarding house for an extended period of time or that she returned to it upon her subsequent visits to Asheville.

Scott and the Asheville Librarian

Although Scott was always somewhat jealous of Tom's recent success, he was quick to come to his friend's defense, even in his own hometown. Ever since the publication of *Look Homeward, Angel* in October of 1929, the story has been told of how the Asheville library where Tom Wolfe spent countless hours as a child had refused to display a copy of the novel on its shelves. Julia Wolfe offered her version to F. Scott Fitzgerald in the summer of 1935:

"Why, they won't even have it in the public library, where he once read every book they had. One day I told Miss Jones, our librarian, it's a shame his books are in all the libraries in the world but his own. She shrugged her shoulders and said Asheville was too poor to buy them. Humph! I know they have them, but under lock and key, and they only let their friends read them. Else how would they know he said those things to make them all sore at him?" – After the Good Gay Times

A later report stated that one of the Asheville librarians was not amused when Tom described her as "hefty" in *Look Homeward, Angel* and for that reason did not place the novel on the public shelves.

Scott, c. 1937. *(Photo courtesy and © by Princeton University Library.)*

In 1953, George W. McCoy, a friend and an editor at the *Asheville Citizen*, wrote:

"In 1929 the librarian borrowed a copy of Look Homeward, Angel, *read portions of it, did not like it, and did not put it on the acquisitions list. When prospective readers called for the book at the circulation desk the reply was: 'I'm sorry, we do not have it.'*

For six years the library remained without a book by Wolfe. Notice of this was taken by Phillips Russell, then an associate professor of English at the University of North Carolina, in a speech he delivered at a banquet held by the North Carolina Library Association in the Battery Park Hotel in Asheville on October 11, 1935. 'I understand that in his home town,' he said, 'the public library has not yet admitted one copy of his books.'

Not long after Professor Russell's speech, F. Scott Fitzgerald, the author, called at Pack Library to borrow a copy of Look Homeward, Angel. *When he was told it did not have one, he walked out, went to a book store, purchased two copies of the book, and presented them to the library. They were accepted, cataloged, and placed in open circulation."*

The record was further annotated by Myra Champion, one of the first Asheville reference librarians to herald the work of Thomas Wolfe. In 1947 she began assembling Pack Library's extensive collection of Thomas Wolfe material and continued amassing it for a quarter of a century. In a 1984 interview with biographer Joanne Marshall Mauldlin, she recalled:

"Miss Anne was one of those straight-laced librarians. She told me, 'You know, Myra, I didn't approve of Thomas Wolfe. I didn't then and I don't now.'

There's no question about it: from 1929 until 1936, no copies of Look Homeward, Angel *were ever in circulation. Miss Anne was head of the library, you see. I later tried to get information out of the library board. Nobody was willing to admit anything. Miss Anne told me the tale that . . . Fitzgerald said he wanted to see a copy of* Look Homeward, Angel. *She told him, 'No, there isn't a copy.' He went downstairs and bought two copies and put them on the circulation desk."*

Saving the Old Kentucky Home –
A Second Time

On July 24, 1998, during an Asheville street festival, an arsonist set fire to the outside of the Old Kentucky Home. The dry wood framing quickly ignited, sending flames up into the attic, causing the roof to collapse. The combination of flames, smoke, and water destroyed nearly a quarter of the original house and approximately two hundred items. The room which suffered the worst damage was the dining room, as all of the doors, windows, flooring, and furniture had been destroyed. Afterwards one individual described it as a "black cave with water dripping all over the place."

The next day the first of hundreds of volunteers, including trained preservationists from the Biltmore Estate, the Carl Sandburg Home, and the National Park Service, began arriving to undertake the laborious task of removing, identifying, storing, and restoring more than six hundred artifacts. The house was covered with an enormous tarp to protect what remained.

The next four years were consumed with negotiations with insurance companies, along with fund-raising events for the extensive restoration process. The final two years of the

Fire, 1994. (Thomas Wolfe Collection, Pack Library, Asheville.)

six-year effort saw the destroyed rooms and roof rebuilt, as well as the furniture refinished, and the entire house cleaned and refurbished. The total cost exceeded $2.4 million, all but $300,000 of which was covered by the insurance policies. No one was ever charged with the crime.

During the time the interior of the house was being restored, the staff continued to provide tours around the grounds and arranged for educational programs in the Visitor Center. The official re-opening took place over Memorial Day Weekend in 2004. The site now averages approximately 20,000 visitors each year.

2. Woodfin House

c. 1881 (demolished 1955)
92 Woodfin Street   W.O. Wolfe, builder

Directions: The site of the original Wolfe family home at 92 Woodfin Street bears a small commemorative marker located on the second level of the YMCA parking lot, located directly east of the building's main entrance. To reach it, walk or drive north one-half block from the Thomas Wolfe Memorial to Woodfin Street. Turn right (east) and go fifty yards, turning into the first driveway leading into the YMCA parking lot. The granite marker is fifty yards from Woodfin Street on the second parking level. It can be found beneath a maple tree beside the second set of concrete stairs connecting the two parking levels. Inscribed on the brass plaque is the following:

Thomas Clayton Wolfe   A Great American Writer
Born On This Site   92 Woodfin Street   October 3, 1900

Walking Time from the Visitor Center: Approximately five minutes.

Woodfin House.   *(Thomas Wolfe Collection, Pack Memorial Library, Asheville, NC.)*

W.O. Wolfe (1851-1922) and his second wife, Cynthia (1842-1884), arrived in Asheville in 1880, having left Raleigh under a cloud of suspicion and scandal. Trained as a stonemason, Wolfe soon established himself as a fine carver of tombstones. Before long he began building a home for his new wife on a lot at 92 Woodfin Street.

"With his great hands he had laid the foundations, burrowed out deep musty cellars in the earth, and sheeted the tall sides over with smooth trowelings of warm brown plaster. He had very little money, but his strange house grew to the rich modelling of his fantasy: when he had finished he had something which leaned to the slope of his narrow uphill yard, something with a high embracing front porch, and warm rooms where one stepped up and down to the tackings of his whim."

— Look Homeward, Angel

A few years later the frail Cynthia, nine years older than her husband, succumbed to tuberculosis on February 22, 1884. She was just 42. Eleven months later, on January 14, 1885, the 34-year-old W.O. married Julia Westall, a 25-year-old school teacher from a well-known Asheville family. Julia moved into his home on Woodfin Street, still decorated with the deceased Cynthia Wolfe's furnishings.

The house at 92 Woodfin Street was much smaller than it appears in period photographs. In truth it had only three bedrooms to be shared by W.O., Julia, and their seven children, all of whom were born in the house. When Tom was born in 1900, the other six Wolfe children were Effie (13), Frank (12), Mabel (10), twins Grover (8) and Ben (8), and Fred (6). They found space wherever they could. Tom slept in his mother's bed at the Woodfin Street house and at the Old Kentucky Home, where Julia moved in 1906, until he was eight years old.

In 1914 W.O. Wolfe was diagnosed with prostate cancer; in 1917 he finally moved out of the Woodfin House and into one of the bedrooms at the Old Kentucky Home boarding house, where he died in 1922. Once all of their children had grown up, Julia had no use for the house W.O. had built for Cynthia, so she sold it in 1920. The house remained outside the Wolfe family for the remainder of its history. By 1955 it had deteriorated badly. Its owner, H.D. Miles, unsuccessfully offered it for sale for $8,500. The fledgling Thomas Wolfe Memorial Association, formed in 1949, had all it could do to keep the Old Kentucky Home open. The consensus seemed to be that trying to restore, maintain, and operate two houses as historical sites might well lead to the demise of both. To the dismay of many people, the Wolfe family home was demolished in 1955. The playhouse which W.O. had built in 1900, however, was carefully relocated in the yard of the Old Kentucky Home.

Orange Street School

1888 (demolished 1939)
71 Orange Street

Directions: The Orange Street School no longer exists, but once stood two blocks north of the corner of Woodfin Street and Central Avenue. All of the Wolfe children attended it, including Tom from 1906 through 1912. In *Look Homeward, Angel* he called it the Plum Street School.

The Orange Street School opened in 1888 at 71 Orange Street as the second public school in Asheville. The impressive, two-and-a-half story brick building featured corner pyramid spires and large arched windows and main doorway. The first floor served the elementary grades, while the second-floor classrooms were earmarked for high school students.

Orange Street School

In September of 1906 Tom reportedly followed his neighborhood friend Max Israel to the Orange Street School. Although Tom was still a month shy of his sixth birthday, the first-grade teacher, Elizabeth Bernard, allowed him to enroll. He still had his shoulder-length curls, which his mother would not cut until he was eight, and only then because a legion of head-lice had invaded the school. Despite some schoolyard taunting by the older boys, Tom seemed to enjoy school, impressing the faculty with his voracious reading ability and his aptitude for memorizing poetry. As an adult, Tom's handwriting was atrocious, as every typist, editor, and proof-reader would later complain. Among the first to point this out to him was his third-grade teacher at the Orange Street School, who noted on his composition, "Your writing is very poor."

The Orange Street School saw limited use after 1930 and was demolished after being condemned in 1939.

Pack Square

Directions: From the entrance to the Thomas Wolfe Memorial Visitor Center, walk south on Market Street, crossing Walnut Street and College Street, going toward the distinct fifteen-story, terracotta, brick, and limestone Jackson Building. It is a privately-owned office building located at the corner of Market Street and Pack Square. The 1924 Jackson Building stands atop the site formerly occupied by W.O. Wolfe's tombstone shop.

Walking Time: Five minutes.

Best Vantage Point: Standing in Pack Square Park diagonally from the Jackson Building is the best place to study the surrounding structures.

From his mother's boarding house where Tom lived from 1906 until he departed for the University of North Carolina in 1916, it was just a three-block walk up the hill to Pack Square, the city's commercial district with various local businesses and his father's shop (center, lowest building).

Pack Square looking east c. 1910.   (North Carolina Collection, Pack Memorial Library, Asheville.)

"Light came and went and came again, the great plume of the fountain pulsed and the winds of April sheeted it across the square, in rainbow gossamer of spray. The fire department horses drummed on the floors with wooden stomp, most casually,

and with dry whiskings of their clean coarse tails. The street cars ground into the square from every portion of the compass and halted briefly like wound toys in their old familiar quarter-hourly formula of assembled Eight. And a dray, hauled by a boneyard nag, rattled across the cobbles on the other side before his father's shop."

– Look Homeward, Angel

Prior to 1906, the commercial center of Asheville was known as Court Square, as it had always been dominated by a succession of Buncombe County courthouses. Later that year, as Tom turned six, the city council voted to rename Court Square in honor of George Willis Pack, a highly successful lumber merchant and philanthropist.

A New York native, the 53-year-old George Pack (1831-1906) visited Asheville in 1884 and immediately made the city his second home, hoping the mountain air would prove beneficial to his ailing wife. Pack reportedly disliked the daily cluster and clutter of horse-drawn wagons and country traders encircling the old courthouse, at that time located on the grassy slope directly in front of the present-day courthouse and city building. He donated four acres of land for a new courthouse, provided city officials would then demolish the existing courthouse to enlarge Court Square.

Prior to his death in 1906, George Pack donated hundreds of thousands of dollars to worthy causes, including providing the land, building, and salaries for a free kindergarten, undertaking much of the cost of the Governor Zebulon Baird Vance obelisk

George Pack. (North Carolina Collection, Pack Memorial Library, Asheville.)

monument at the west end of the Square, providing a building on the square to serve as a new public library, and donating funds for the YMCA, various hospitals, and several city parks. Nearly all of his donations were made quietly, without fanfare or in need of public acknowledgment, often simply with a note attached to the check.

During Tom Wolfe's childhood, the north, west, and south sides of Pack Square consisted primarily of two-story and three-story brick buildings housing a variety of businesses facing the square's fountain and the Vance Memorial monument.

31.

3. W. O. Wolfe Tombstone Shop

c.1890 (demolished 1923)
22 South Pack Square
William Oliver Wolfe, builder

William Oliver Wolfe was born on April 10, 1851, near York Springs, Pennsylvania, midway between Harrisburg and Gettysburg. In 1865 W.O. Wolfe traveled to Baltimore to practice the trade of stonecutting. Upon hearing of the need for stonecutters to work on a new state penitentiary in Raleigh, in 1871 he moved to North Carolina, where he soon opened his own shop. After a failed first marriage and a scandalous affair, he wed Cynthia C. Hill, nine years his senior. In 1880 the couple moved to Asheville. Cynthia, however, died from tuberculosis at age forty-two on February 22, 1884. At that time Wolfe was leasing a shop on the north side of the square.

"He was only past thirty, but he looked much older. His face was yellow and sunken; the waxen blade of his nose looked like a beak. He had long brown mustaches that hung straight down mournfully. His tremendous bouts of drinking had wrecked his health. He was thin as a rail and had a cough. He thought he had tuberculosis and that he was going to die." – Look Homeward, Angel

Just eleven months later, on January 14, 1885, W.O. married Julia Westall (1860-1945), a 25-year-old school teacher from a well-known Asheville family. As she reminisced, "When I married Mr. Wolfe, he had this home, and he rented his marble shop. He did not pay very much rent and it was out of what he earned that I wanted him to buy a lot up in the building section of the town and build a business."

"From the savings of her small wage as teacher and book-agent, she had already

Shop far left. (Thomas Wolfe Collection, Pack Memorial Library, Asheville, NC.)

purchased one or two pieces of earth. On one of these, a small lot at the edge of the public square, she persuaded him to build a shop. This he did with his own hands, and the labor of two Negro men: it was a two-story shack of brick, with wide wooden steps, leading down to the square from a marble porch. Upon this porch, flanking the wooden doors, he placed some marbles; by the door, he put the heavy simpering figure of an angel." – Look Homeward, Angel

Despite his ongoing and ineffective battle with alcoholism, which resulted in numerous public and private drunken outbursts, W.O. Wolfe remained a skilled craftsman, as biographer David H. Donald documented, "He made a good enough living from his tombstones so that the Wolfe family was better off than nine out of ten families in Asheville. A skilled craftsman, he lettered inscriptions with precision, and he had a talent for carving little lambs, or hands folded in prayer, on his monuments. Occasionally he sold one of the seven-foot funerary angels, made of Carrara marble, which he had accepted on consignment and displayed on the porch outside his shop. But what he made he spent freely, on himself and on his family."

From the time he could walk until he left for the University of North Carolina in 1916, Tom often wandered up to his father's stonecutting shop on the busy square. Photographs reveal a modest shop cluttered with an assortment of granite tombstones, samples for people

W.O. Wolfe, right.   (*Thomas Wolfe Collection, Pack Memorial Library, Asheville, NC.*)

to view, as well as those into which W.O. was presently carving names, dates, and inscriptions for the recently deceased.

"Between the workroom and the ware-room, on the left as one entered, was Gant's office, a small room, deep in the dust of twenty years with an old-fashioned desk, sheaves of banded dirty papers, a leather sofa, a smaller desk layered with round and square samples of marble and granite. The dirty window, which was never opened, looked out on the sloping market square, pocketed obliquely off the public Square."
– Look Homeward, Angel

Despite the criticism Tom often leveled at his father through the pseudo-fictitious characters of Eugene and his father William Oliver Gant, the young author reveals a deep respect for W.O. Wolfe's high level of craftsmanship:

"He would find his father in the workroom, bending over a trestle, using the heavy wooden mallet with delicate care, as he guided the chisel through the mazes of an inscription. He never wore work-clothes; he worked dressed in well brushed garments of heavy black, his coat removed, and a long-striped apron covering all his front."

"As Eugene saw him, he felt that this was no common craftsman, but a master, picking up his tools briefly for a chef-d'oeuvre. "He is better at this than anyone in all the world," Eugene thought, and his dark vision burned in him for a moment, as he thought that his father's work would never, as men reckon years, be extinguished."
– Look Homeward, Angel

W.O. Wolfe   *(Thomas Wolfe Collection, Pack Memorial Library, Asheville, NC.)*

By 1917 the combined effects of the cancer and arthritis in his hands, wrists, and arms made it difficult for W.O. Wolfe to continue working. As a result, in 1920 he and Julia sold the two-story tombstone shop for $25,000. Most of his final two years of life were spent in one of the second-floor bedrooms in his wife's boarding house, where Julia Wolfe and their daughter Mabel cared for him. On June 20, 1922, after more than five years of painful suffering, 71-year old William Oliver Wolfe succumbed to prostate cancer.

3. Jackson Building

1924
22 South Pack Square
Ronald Greene, architect

In 1923 the former Wolfe tombstone building was again sold, this time to real estate developer Lynwood B. Jackson, who proceeded to have the building razed. Despite the fact that the lot at the corner of Market Street and Pack Square measured just 25 feet wide by 62 feet deep, Jackson commissioned Asheville architect Ronald Greene (1891-1961) to design Asheville's first true skyscraper on it. The fifteen-story, steel and terracotta skyscraper was completed in 1924. It is reported to hold the record for the tallest building on the smallest lot.

Jackson, Westall, and Commerce Buildings.
(North Carolina Collection, Pack Memorial Library, Asheville.)

At the time of its completion, Asheville was in a real estate frenzy and building boom, enabling Jackson to fully lease the skyscraper even before it opened. By then Asheville's population had increased to nearly 30,000 residents and was visited annually by an estimated 250,000 people. To draw tourists to his Neo-Gothic roof-top observatory, Jackson installed a powerful searchlight and 400-power telescope.

The observation tower at the top, no longer open to the public, has sometimes been erroneously referred to as a "bell tower," but L.B. Jackson never intended to have a bell installed in it. In a similar manner, what are often misnamed "gargoyles" near the top of the building are actually projecting stone "grotesques" – the architectural term for a carved mythological or imaginary figure solely intended as a decorative element on a building. To be a gargoyle it must direct water off the roof and onto the ground, which would have proven dangerous to pedestrians twelve stories below.

In one of its more unique functions, L.B. Jackson allowed city officials to assign an officer to the top of the fifteen-story structure to serve as a "clean air lookout." If one of the hundreds of coal-burning furnaces in downtown Asheville emitted dark, heavy smoke for more than five minutes, the lookout would issue a warning to the owner to have the furnace repaired to burn more efficiently.

According to Wolfe's biographer Elizabeth Nowell, before leaving Asheville on September 2, 1937, "one of the last things he did was to go to the office of a friend [J.Y. Jordan] high up in the town's modern skyscraper, the Jackson Building, built on the site of Mr. Wolfe's own tombstone shop, and to stride from window to window, gazing at the mountains that encircle Asheville as though he might never set eyes on them again."

In the years since its opening, the Jackson Building has inspired more than a few unsubstantiated stories. Local tour guides enjoy suggesting that the building is haunted by the ghost of a man who some people claim jumped to his death during the depths of the Great Depression. Some even go so far as to point out that the contemporary circle of decorative concrete and brick outside the Jackson Building marks the spot where the man died. Neither claim has ever been substantiated. A marker commemorating W.O. Wolfe and his shop stands in front of the Jackson Building, consisting of two granite slabs, one topped with a stonecutter's tools. Today the Jackson Building serves as a private office building and is not open to the public.

4. Fire Station #1

1926   100 Pack Square
Ronald Greene, architect

After a pressurized water system was installed in 1887, the city purchased their first team of horses to pull a new hose wagon. The horses, reportedly named Tom and Dick, lived in stables beside the courthouse. According to local historians, Tom and Dick were trained to listen for the sound of the fire bell, followed by the release of a chain across the front of their stalls. The horses then calmly walked to their assigned positions in front of the hose wagon, where they stood and waited until their driver arrived to lower their harnesses, suspended from the ceiling.

As a child, Tom Wolfe would have stepped out of his father's tombstone shop on the site of the present-day Jackson Building to watch the team of horses race up Pack Square:

"The firemen loved to stage the most daring exhibitions before the gaping citizenry; helmeted magnificently, they hung from the wagons in gymnastic postures, one man holding another over rushing space, while number two caught in mid-air the diving heavy body of the Swiss, who deliberately risked his neck as he leaped for the rail. Thus, for one rapturous moment they stood poised triangularly over rocking speed: the spine of the town was chilled ecstatically." – Look Homeward, Angel

As the city grew, so did the need for a larger fire station and a full-time staff of firefighters. Designed by Asheville architect Ronald Greene, the new $100,000 fire station opened to great fanfare on March 8, 1926. Built on a gentle slope, the structure is actually four stories tall at the back. It originally housed the fire department, the police department, a courtroom, and a city jail. In addition, it included sleeping quarters, a kitchen, a reading room, a lounge area, a gymnasium, and three fire poles.

On the night of August 18, 1937, two Asheville police officers came upon an inebriated Thomas Wolfe, who had just returned from testifying in a murder trial in Burnsville. Rather than filing charges against him, officers Glenn Tweed and J.G. Anderson let him sleep it off in the city jail, which was then inside what is now Fire Station #1. Had he been brought to court the following morning, Tom would have stood before Judge Sam Cathey, who had attended the University of North Carolina at the same time as Wolfe. He and Tom shared a passion for professional baseball, as Wolfe was a devoted follower of the New York Yankees.

5. Sky Club Building

(Currently the Sky Club Condominiums)
181 Ardmion Park   Beaucatcher Mountain
Oliver Cromwell Hamilton, original owner   1896

Looking down upon the city of Asheville from the western slope of Beaucatcher Mountain is the stately three-story, six-column Sky Club Building. Constructed in 1896 by Oliver Cromwell Hamilton, a wealthy Chicago banker, it served as his family's home until he lost his fortune in the Stock Market Crash of 1929. It was then purchased by Gus and Emma Adler and transformed into a restaurant and dance club. Over the years it has undergone a number of name changes: the Castle, the Sky Club, the

Old Heidelberg Supper Club, the Castle in the Sky, the Satellite Club and, most recently, the Sky Club Condominiums at Ardmion Park. During prohibition, the supper club's patrons would bring their own liquor, paying Gus and Emma one dollar for a bucket of ice.

Around August 23, 1937, during his two-month stay at what is now referred to as the Wolfe Cabin, Tom, who never had a driver's license, asked a friend to drive him up to the Sky Club. Upon dropping him off, Wolfe reportedly said to come back and pick him up in the morning. When he returned after dawn, he found Tom and a group of new friends still engaged in heated conversation at a table littered with cigarette butts and empty bottles. While the two authors never drank there together, the Sky Club was also one of F. Scott Fitzgerald's favorite bars when he stayed in the city in 1935 and 1936.

6. Asheville City Building

1928
70 Court Plaza
Douglas Ellington, architect

7. Buncombe County Courthouse

1928
60 Court Plaza
Milburn, Heister and Company, architects

In 1927, a war broke out in Asheville. It was fought entirely in conference rooms, around coffee shops, and on the editorial pages of the local newspapers. The foes were supporters of fashionable Art Deco versus those who favored the more conservative Neo-Classical architecture.

A few years earlier Asheville had joined the rest of the country in a post-war building frenzy which lasted from 1919 until the silent crash heard around the world on October 29, 1929. During that time more than sixty-five buildings were constructed in downtown Asheville. In 1926, as the townspeople watched in amazement, local brickmasons transformed architect Douglas Ellington's blueprints for an Art Deco place of worship into the unorthodox First Baptist Church.

Riding a wave of popularity, Ellington was approached by the Asheville City Council and the Buncombe County Commissioners who asked him to design a matching City Building, County Courthouse, and covered arcade connecting the two towering structures. It was a proposal which would have propelled Asheville to prominence alongside Miami in Art Deco architectural excellence.

Ellington's intent was to create two complimentary structures in which "the contours of the building reflect the mountain background and that the building be equally presentable from all points of view." Upon its completion in 1928, Asheville city officials proclaimed that "no finer municipal building existed anywhere in the United States."

As it was going up, however, county officials began to have second thoughts. As one county commissioner loudly protested, "Who the hell ever heard of a courthouse without columns?" Instead, the county commissioners reached outside Asheville, ignoring a legion of talented area architects, placing responsibility for the design of a courthouse in the hands of Milburn, Heister and Company in Washington, DC. As Ellington predicted, "the result will inevitably be nothing more than two separate structures unrelated, inharmonious, [and] misplaced . . . ."

Buncombe County Courthouse.   *Asheville City Building.*

(North Carolina Collection, Pack Memorial Library, Asheville.)

As many feared, the county commissioners favored a traditional, conservative courthouse design. No one questioned the reputation nor the experience of Milburn, Heister and Company in designing an adequate courthouse. They only feared the two contrasting styles of architecture in two government buildings located mere yards apart would strike

39.

a jarring chord. Adding salt to the wound was the fact that while Douglas Ellington's proposed design for a complimentary Art Deco city building and courthouse could have both been built for total of $1.5 million, the seventeen-story Neo-Classical County Courthouse alone ended up costing taxpayers $2.5 million.

While Tom Wolfe would not have seen either the City Building or the County Courthouse while growing up, he would have seen them on his trips back to Asheville in 1928, 1929, and again in 1937.

As author Richard Hansley observed of the City Building, "Taking the principles of Art Deco styling and blending it with classical motifs, Ellington created a building that has stood the test of time and is as breathtaking in concept and appearance today as it was when completed."

Despite both buildings now being more than ninety years old, they continue to function today, although additional office and jail space has recently been secured. And while each building stands as a proud representative of its own distinct and contrasting architectural style, one can't help but stand, stare, and wonder, "What if . . . ?"

Pack Square:
The South, West and North Sides

From the age of six until at sixteen he left for the University of North Carolina, Tom Wolfe escaped the turmoil of his mother's boarding house by walking to Pack Square. There he spent time in his father's tombstone shop before making his way across Pack Square, walking toward his two favorite places: the public library and the North State Fitting school.

Directions: From the Jackson Building proceed along the south side of Pack Square, going past the Westall Building, the Commerce Building, and the Legal Building to the plaza in front of the Asheville Art Museum.

Walking Time: Less than five minutes.

8. Westall Building

1924
20 South Pack Square
Ronald Greene, architect

Under a somewhat unusual arrangement, successful Asheville business-man William A. Westall, who was the younger brother of Julia Westall Wolfe, hence an uncle to Tom Wolfe, partnered with Asheville develop-er L.B. Jackson to construct two unique, yet conjoined buildings on the former site of the Wolfe tombstone shop. The men both hired Asheville architect Ronald Greene to design their structures.

Early in their discussions, the two buildings on Pack Square were intended to be Gothic twins, but in their final form they differ significant-ly. The eight-story Westall Building favored Greene's blend of Spanish Romanesque and English Norman detailing, especially around the top, while the taller Jackson Building remained a stellar example of Greene's interpretation of Neo-Gothic architecture.

Adding to the uniqueness of the arrangement, the two owners and Ronald Greene agreed that the buildings would share an elevator to be located inside the Jackson Building, giving the eight-story Westall Building the distinction of being one of the tallest office buildings ever constructed without an elevator (pictured, pg. 35).

9. Commerce Building

1904
18 South Pack Square

In 1904 the modest, brick three-story Commerce Building was construct-ed at 18 South Pack Square, just a few feet from the W.O. Wolfe tomb-stone shop then standing on the corner of Pack Square and Market Street. The Commerce Building survived the rash of demolitions in downtown Asheville which took place prior to the Stock Market Crash of 1929. It continues to serve as an office building today.

10. Legal Building

1909   10 South Pack Square
Richard Sharpe Smith, architect

Standing next to the Commerce Building is the monumental five-story Legal Building, designed in 1909 by Richard Sharpe Smith (1852-1924), Asheville's most prolific architect. It was one of the first buildings in the city to be constructed of poured concrete. It once housed the Central Bank and Trust Company, Asheville's largest bank, which failed in 1930, costing the city of Asheville millions of dollars in lost assets.

On February 25, 1931, former Asheville mayor Gallatin Roberts, who had authorized the transfer of nearly all of the city's funds into the Central Bank and Trust Company, committed suicide in a fourth-floor restroom. A grand jury investigation later absolved Roberts of any fraud charges. The bank's failure also cost Roberts his family's entire savings.

The five-story Legal Building can be seen to the left of the Vance Monument. The "castle" to the right is the former library frequented by young Tom Wolfe before it was demolished.
(North Carolina Collection, Pack Memorial Library, Asheville.)

11. Asheville Art Museum

East Section: 1926   Edward L. Tilton, architect
West Section: 2019   Ennead Architects

The south side of Pack Square has always consisted of a blend of architectural styles, "that hodgepodge of ill-sorted architectures," as Thomas Wolfe described it.

The 2019 glass-faced modern Asheville Art Museum adjoins the marble historic Pack Memorial Library building, designed in 1926 by New York architect Edward L. Tilton (1861-1933), who specialized in libraries and educational buildings across the country. In 1978, after a new public library was constructed five blocks away, the three-story building became the home of the Asheville Art Museum.

The 1926 Pack Memorial Library building still standing on Pack Square was not the one frequented by Tom Wolfe as a child, as that first library was demolished during the downtown building frenzy of the 1920s. Pack Memorial Library was, however, the infamous library which for years refused to place a copy of *Look Homeward, Angel* on its shelves.

When Tom was in second grade, his father reportedly walked him up the street from his stonemason shop to the public library, where he registered Tom for a library card. From then on, Tom typically would leave school and walk to the library on Pack Square. The librarian, Grace Jones, reported that, "Tom had read more books than any boy in North Carolina,

and he doesn't stick to children's books. He reads everything."

In 1983 the United Daughters of the Confederacy, Chapter 104, commissioned the University of North Carolina at Asheville professor and sculptor Dan Millspaugh to create the "Thomas Wolfe Memorial Angel," which stands on the site of the original public library. The bronze statue was unveiled in a ceremony held in front of the 1926 former Pack Memorial Library on October 3, 1983. It closely resembles the Wolfe angel in Hendersonville's Oakdale Cemetery (see entry).

(Photo courtesy of CityData.com.)

43.

12. Pack Square: West Side

The southwest corner of Pack Square still includes a number of structures dating back to 1887. They survived a disastrous fire in 1895 which had prompted a rebuilding of several businesses in this area. These buildings exhibit classic architectural detailing which Tom Wolfe would have seen almost daily on his walks to his father's tombstone shop and to the North State Fitting School, including decorative cornices, corbels, rock lintels, quarried sandstone piers, arched windows, terracotta features, and double hung windows.

West Side of Pack Square, c.1900.   (*North Carolina Collection, Pack Memorial Library, Asheville.*)

Pack Square: North Side

13. Biltmore Building

1 North Pack Square
I.M. Pei and Partners   1980

The entire row of two- and three-story brick buildings which once lined the north side of Pack Square was demolished in 1977 to make room for the gleaming, seven-story office building built in 1980 by the Akzona Corporation, a textile manufacturer. Designed by the internationally-respected firm of I.M. Pei and Partners, it was purchased by the Biltmore Company in 1986 and is now known as the Biltmore Building.

14. Vance Monument

1897-1898

Central Pack Square Plaza   Richard Sharpe Smith, designer

The most well-known politician to have come out of Asheville was Zebulon Baird Vance (1830-1894). He served as a colonel in the Confederate army for one year, then was elected governor of North Carolina in 1862 and 1864. After the war Vance reopened his law practice in Charlotte before again being elected as governor in 1876 and as a United States senator in 1879. He was still serving as senator when he died in 1894 at the age of 64. Family disputes afterwards resulted in Vance being buried three different times in Riverside Cemetery.

In 1896 George Pack donated $2,000 toward a monument in Vance's honor, a 75-foot tall obelisk of rough-hewn granite designed by architect Richard Sharpe Smith (1852-1924), an English-born architect who had arrived in Asheville in 1889 to supervise construction of the 1889-1895 Biltmore House.

On the night of November 13, 1906, a criminal by the name of Will Harris killed two policemen and three people near Pack Square. One of the bullets fired during the exchange reportedly struck the Vance Monument, but any result-

(N.C. Collection, Pack Memorial Library, Asheville.)

ing chip has become impossible to distinguish. The incident inspired Thomas Wolfe to write a short story entitled "The Child by Tiger."

In 2002 the City of Asheville completed the Urban Trail, a self-guided walking tour highlighted by thirty stations. At the base of the Vance Monument stands the statues of two bronze turkeys and two bronze pigs walking along a replica of the Buncombe Turnpike. The iron rails beside them were originally part of the trolley system which operated in Asheville until 1934.

Patton Avenue and Church Street

At the age of twelve, Tom Wolfe enrolled in a new private preparatory school owned by teachers John and Margaret Roberts, who first called it the North State Fitting School. To reach the Roberts' home from his mother's boarding house, Tom would have walked up Market Street to Pack Square. He would have then turned west, walking past the Vance Monument and down Patton Avenue toward Church Street, two blocks away. While the North State Fitting School has since been demolished, the route along Patton Avenue and Church Street is lined with architectural landmarks.

Directions: From either the Asheville Art Museum or the Vance Monument walk west along either side of Patton Avenue, crossing Lexington Avenue and continuing one more block until reaching Church Street.

Time: Approximately five minutes.

15. Kress Building

1928

19 Patton Avenue   E.J.T. Hoffman, architect

One block west of the Vance Monument, at the intersection of Patton and Lexington Avenues, stands the restored four-story Kress Building. While it was not built during Tom Wolfe's childhood, he undoubtedly would have seen it, perhaps even walked through it, on his trips back to Asheville in the summers of 1928, 1929, and again in 1937.

Designed by the firm's staff architect, E.J.T. Hoffman (active 1918-1928), the S.H. Kress Company built one of its finest five-and-dime stores in Asheville in 1928. Samuel Henry Kress had opened his first five-and-dime store in Memphis in 1896 and rose to become a chief rival of the F.W. Woolworth Company with more than 300 stores across the country.

In addition to being a savvy merchandiser, Samuel Kress appreciated architecture and collected fine art. He was unique in that he always maintained a staff architect who designed each Kress store for him. In 1918 Samuel Kress promoted E.J.T. Hoffman to the position of chief architect. Over the next ten years, the prolific Hoffman designed 49 stores for Kress, increasing their number of stores from 144 to 193. Hoffman was noted for many innovative features which gave Kress stores a high degree of elegance, including ornate plaster columns, mirrored piers, marble veneers, and nighttime lighting. The Asheville store is considered by architectural historians to represent Hoffman's finest example of his work for Samuel Kress.

Like many historic Kress buildings across the country, the Kress Building in Asheville has been recognized for its architectural significance and has since been preserved and restored. Today the ground floor serves as a retail space, while the upper three floors have been converted into condominiums.

16. Drhumor Building

1896
48 Patton Avenue
Allen L. Melton, architect   Frederick B. Miles, sculptor

On his way to the North State Fitting School, Tom would have turned south off Patton Avenue and onto Church Street. At the intersection he would have passed beneath the elaborately carved Drhumor (pronounced Dru'-moor) Building, designed in 1896 by architect Allen L. Melton.

Allen L. Melton (1852-1917) moved to Asheville as a 34-year-old architect at a time when the city was experiencing its first building boom after the arrival of the railroad in 1880. Within a few years Melton had established himself as a popular and prolific architect willing to work in a variety of styles. One ad offered to provide drawings for "Colleges, Churches, Court Houses, Jails, & Private Buildings of Every Description."

In 1895 real estate developer William Johnston Cocke commissioned Melton to design this four-story commercial building on a downtown lot he had recently inherited. Cocke, who was descended from a family of Irish politicians, named the building after his grandfather's ancestral estate in Ireland. Designed in the popular Romanesque Revival style with arched windows and limestone trim, Melton's original entrance faced the corner of the intersection, but the doorway was later converted to windows when a new entrance was designed on Patton Avenue.

Melton and Cocke selected Frederick B. Miles (1860-1921) to design and carve the elaborate first-floor frieze. Born in England and trained as a stonecutter and sculptor, Miles learned the craft of stonecutting from his father prior to enrolling in the School of Art in South Kensington. In 1891 he brought his wife and children to Asheville, as he had secured a position as a stone carver and sculptor for George Vanderbilt's Biltmore House, where he worked with architect Richard Sharpe Smith from 1891 until 1895.

The unique frieze features a wide variety of richly-carved figures, forms, and decorative detailing, including mythological characters, animals, plants, winged mermaids and angels, doves, Masonic and Freemasonry symbols, a blacksmith at his anvil, and at least twenty human faces. According to legend, Miles used some of his friends as models for the faces, but time has eclipsed any accurate record of their association.

Tom Wolfe had not forgotten the familiar Drhumor Building when writing about his hometown in *Look Home-ward, Angel*. This descriptive passage, however, was deleted from the final version, as editor Maxwell Perkins searched for ways to reduce the bulk of the original gigantic manuscript:

Drhumor Building. (North Carolina Collection, Pack Memorial Library, Asheville.)

"At the corner of Church Street, the somber but lofty grandeur of the Grindle Build-ing beetles down upon him . . . the edifice, a pleasing blend of architectural motifs of the late Victorian and middle-dynastic Egyptian periods, unites beauty with utility in such a way that neither the eye of the most fastidious nor the observation of the most practical can find fault with their happy marriage."

"Constructed originally of piss-colored limestone, the edifice had submitted grate-fully to the kiss of Altamont's incomparable seasons and now has the mellow amber weathering of deep-hued dung."

Church Street

From 1912 until the fall of 1916, Tom would have turned south off Patton Avenue on his walk to the North State Fitting School at 157 Church Street. While no evidence remains of the school, four buildings of architectural and historical significance line the first three blocks, including the church where Thomas Wolfe's funeral was held in 1938.

Directions: Turn south down Church Street on either side of the street, passing Commerce Street and Aston Street.

Walking Time: Approximately five minutes.

17. First Bank - Asheville Savings Bank Building

1922, 1965, 2005
11 Church Street
Ronald Greene, architect

One block down Church Street stands what, until recently, had for decades been known as the Asheville Savings Bank Building. In 1922 Asheville architect Ronald Greene (1891-1961) was commissioned to redesign three existing separate buildings into one cohesive structure in a style influenced by ancient Greek architecture, with Tuscan columns and formal dentil molding. Greene combined the central building with one facing Commerce Street by applying a layer of concrete veneer fabricated to look like actual stone. The third building, which fronts Church Street, retains its original brick surface.

18. Central United Methodist Church

1905, with additions in 1924 and 1967
27 Church Street   Reuben H. Hunt, architect

Young Tom Wolfe would have been quite familiar with the Central United Methodist Church, as he would have passed by it twice daily on school days. The Wolfe family only occasionally attended Sunday services across the street at the First Presbyterian Church, where Thomas Wolfe's funeral was held after his death on September 15, 1938.

Groundbreaking for this, the third Methodist Church at this location, took place in 1902, but it was not until 1905 that the spacious sanctuary and its flanking towers were completed. The congregation selected Chattanooga architect Reuben H. Hunt (1862-1937) as the designer and Asheville's J.M. Westall, Tom Wolfe's uncle, as the contractor.

19. First Presbyterian Church

1885   40 Church Street

Known to be one of the oldest surviving churches in Asheville, the First Presbyterian Church opened its doors in 1885. In 1915, his third year as a student under John and Margaret Roberts, the fifteen-year-old Tom would have watched as the sanctuary was enlarged and Sunday school rooms added. The building underwent a series of renovations in 1951, 1968, and 2003, but has retained its Gothic Revival character.

According to church historians, Julia Wolfe sometimes attended services at the First Presbyterian Church and, when they were young, brought her children as well. Tom reportedly stopped attending as a teenager. As one biographer summarized, "he simply drifted away."

Thomas Wolfe's funeral procession.   (*Thomas Wolfe Collection, Pack Memorial Library, Asheville*)

Funeral services for several members of the Wolfe family, including Tom, were held in this church. After arriving by train from Baltimore where he died on September 15, 1938, Tom's metal casket was placed in the parlor of the Old Kentucky Home. "He looked so handsome in death, like a marble statue," a friend recalled. Biographer Joanne Marshall Mauldlin wrote, "Wolfe lay in his blue suit with a rose in his lapel. The black wig was slightly askew on his shaved skull. His cheeks were rouged. By all accounts Wolfe's hands, although nicotine stained, were beautiful."

On Sunday, September 18, his body was driven from the Old Kentucky Home to the First Presbyterian Church. Thirty minutes before the 3:00pm funeral, the sanctuary, the balcony, and the lawn were filled to capacity. People lined both sides of Church Street, standing in the shade of the trees in front of the United Methodist Church. An irritated Methodist minister reportedly muttered to one of the pallbearers, "He's not entitled to a Christian burial."

Although retired, Dr. Robert F. Campbell, who had known Tom as a boy, officiated at the funeral, at which he confessed, "I wish I had something definite to say about his religious life." Dr. Campbell had also presided over the funeral services for Grover, Ben, and W.O. Wolfe, and the weddings of Effie and Mabel, but seemed at a loss as to how to handle Tom's service. He read a passage from *Of Time and the River:*

"Where shall the weary rest? Where shall the lonely of heart come home? What doors are open for the wanderer? And which of us shall find his father, know his face, and in what place, and in what time, and in what land? Where? Where the weary of heart can abide forever, where the weary of wandering can find peace, where the tumult, the fever, and the fret shall forever be stilled."

While never capitalized in Tom's manuscript or text, when the *Asheville Citizen-Times* printed the passage the following day, the editor capitalized "Father" and "His face" in a misdirected attempt to instill a deeper religious belief into Tom's life than was accurate.

Hundreds of people, many of whom had been skewered in the pages of *Look Homeward, Angel,* lined the streets of Asheville to view the hearse as it made the slow journey up Church Street, turning left to pass through the business district along Haywood Street on its way to Riverside Cemetery, where another crowd had gathered.

But as another observer wryly noted, "There were thousands who stayed away and hardly knew he was dead. But there were enough to fill the Presbyterian Church and to make it look like the funeral of a prominent local insurance man. We sang lusty hymns."

20. Trinity Episcopal Church

1913
60 Church Street
Bertram Grosvenor Goodhue, architect

Formed in 1849, the original Trinity Episcopal Church was built on this site on land donated by James and Henrietta Patton. That church was replaced in the 1880s with a larger brick building, but it burned to the ground on November 15, 1910, when Tom Wolfe was ten years old. Two years later, as Tom walked along Church Street, he would have watched as brickmasons laid up the walls of the present-day Gothic Revival structure. Designed by famed New York church architect Bertram Grosvenor Goodhue (1869-1924), it was laid upon the stone foundation of the second church. The congregation held its first service there in June of 1913.

The stained-glass windows in the church were designed by New York artist Mary Elizabeth Tillinghast (1855-1912), who had apprenticed under stained glass artist John La Farge before going out on her own. She specialized in church windows, as well as residential designs, and was awarded gold medals at numerous exhibitions. Tragically, she died in December of 1912 at the age of fifty-seven, so was never able to see the installation of her final windows in the Trinity Episcopal Church.

21. North State Fitting School

157 Church Street (demolished)
John and Margaret Roberts
(John and Margaret Leonard, Altamont Fitting School)

Directions: The former site of the first North State Fitting School is three blocks south of the First Presbyterian Church. What had once been a small farm, woods, and house at the edge of Asheville has since been leveled and developed. No marker exists to note the location of the Roberts' experimental school. The ridge and hillside, also known as Buxton Hill, are currently occupied by a number of houses, businesses, and light industrial shops, including Graybar Electric.

Walking Time: Approximately five minutes each way.

In 1912 John Munsey Roberts (1874-1954) and his wife, Margaret Roberts (1876-1947), opened the North State Fitting School. Classes were first held in a large farmhouse at 157 Church Street. As one of their ads read: "Preparation for the best colleges – large and small boys. Individual attention."

North State Fitting School.   *(North Carolina Collection,
Pack Memorial Library, Asheville.)*

Annual tuition at the private school was one hundred dollars, which Julia Wolfe thought too expensive. Tom's father, however, agreed to pay for it, recognizing that his youngest son was destined for college.

While Tom disliked John Roberts' teaching methods, he adored Margaret Roberts, who taught English and guided him toward more literary works. He called her the "mother of my spirit who fed me with light."

"She took him into a big room on the left that had been fitted out as a living-room and library. She watched his face light with eagerness as he saw the fifteen hundred or two thousand books shelved away in various places. He sat down clumsily in a wicker chair by the table and waited until she returned, bringing him a plate of sandwiches and a tall glass of clabber, which he had never tasted before.

'Well, tell me boy,' she said, 'what have you been reading?' Craftily he picked his way across the waste land of printery, naming as his favorites those books which he felt would win her approval. As he had read everything, good and bad, that the town library contained, he was able to make an impressive showing. She was excited and eager – she saw at once how abundantly she could feed this ravenous hunger for knowledge, experience, wisdom." – Look Homeward, Angel

Tom attended the North State Fitting School for four years. In 1916 he announced to the Roberts and his family that he was ready to enroll in college. Although just sixteen, he had hoped to enroll in either Princeton or the University of Virginia, but W.O., who again agreed to pay for his education, insisted that Tom attend the University of North Carolina at Chapel Hill.

"But the school had become the centre of his heart and life – Margaret Leonard his spiritual mother. He liked to be there most in the afternoons when the crowd of boys had gone, and when he was free to wander about the old house, under the singing majesty of great trees, exultant in the proud solitude of that fine hill, the clean windy rain of the acorns, the tang of burning leaves. He would read wolfishly until Margaret discovered him and drove him out under the trees."

– Look Homeward, Angel

Margaret Roberts.

North Carolina Collection, Pack Memorial Library, Asheville.

Sadly, in 1920 the Roberts closed the North State School, as they had renamed it in 1915, and both returned to the public school system. Margaret taught at the Grace High School, where John began serving as principal. Margaret and Tom Wolfe continued to correspond with each other until the release of *Look Homeward, Angel* in October of 1929.

Angered and hurt by Wolfe's caustic portrayal of John Roberts, Margaret refused to answer his letters until 1936. They met briefly during the summer of 1937, but relations remained strained. Margaret, who suffered from stress and latent tuberculosis, died of cancer on May 9, 1947. Her husband John, despite the pain caused them both by *Look Homeward, Angel,* selected a quotation by Tom Wolfe to be chiseled on her tombstone:

"She remained, who first had touched his blinded eyes with light."

John suffered a stroke and died in 1954. Unknown to most visitors, they are buried in Riverside Cemetery, beside each other and not far from the grave of Thomas Wolfe.

Downtown Asheville

When, at the end of a day of classes, young Tom Wolfe left the North State Fitting School on lower Church Street, he might well have taken a more circuitous route back to his domineering mother and the motley band of strangers wandering throughout the boarding house that was his home. Upon reaching the intersection of Church Street and Patton Avenue, rather than turning east back toward Pack Square, he often would have turned west, downtown, toward what is now Pritchard Park and up Haywood Street, until turning east and making his way home.

Directions: From the corner of Church Street and Patton Avenue, continue west, passing in front of the entrances to the Drhumor Building and the S&W Cafeteria. Turn north on Haywood Street, crossing College Avenue and Walnut Street until reaching Vanderbilt Place beside Pack Library.

Walking Time: Less than ten minutes.

22. S & W Cafeteria

1929
56 Patton Avenue
Douglas Ellington, architect   Frank Sherrill, original owner

When they arrived home from World War I, mess sergeants Frank O. Sherrill and Fred Webber decided to open a chain of downtown cafeterias named after their combined initials. Their first was in Charlotte in 1920, soon followed by S&W Cafeterias in Atlanta, Raleigh, Chattanooga, Knoxville, Roanoke, and Asheville. By the time the S&W Cafeteria opened in Asheville in 1929, Sherrill had become sole owner of the thriving business. He commissioned architect Douglas Ellington to design the Patton Avenue cafeteria in the popular Art Deco style. By that time Ellington had also designed the First Baptist Church, the Asheville City Building, and the Asheville High School.

Upon his return to Asheville during the summer of 1937, Tom Wolfe ate several meals here rather than attempting to master the wood-burning cook stove in his rented cabin outside of town.

This famous Art Deco building has become a symbol of downtown Asheville. Intentionally non-symmetrical, the structure features two arched windows framing the entry door sheltered beneath the metal canopy. To the left, then, is what might erroneously be mistaken for an afterthought: another large window, but surrounded this time by a rectangular frame of similar, although not identical terracotta tiles. The row of windows and medallions above the three windows, however, are evenly spaced in a symmetric arrangement.

Well worth noticing is the colorful bowl of ceramic fruit, including grapes, apples, pears, and a banana, Ellington appropriately positioned above the door to the downtown eatery. The entire façade is a study in classic Art Deco detailing, from Egyptian motifs to bandings of geometrical squares, rectangles, trapezoids, circles, and triangles.

S&W Cafeteria.   (North Carolina Collection, Pack Memorial Library, Asheville.)

The S&W Cafeteria closed in 1974, when its owners opened a restaurant in the new Asheville Mall. In 1977 the building was added to the National Register of Historic Places. For several years since then it has struggled to find a business to complement its location and design. Most recently it has served as a restaurant and special events center, with ten condominium units installed in the upper floors.

23. Pritchard Park

1932
Patton Avenue and Haywood Street
Chauncey D. Beadle, landscape architect

When young Tom Wolfe made the turn from Patton Avenue onto Haywood Street, what is now Pritchard Park was then occupied by the United States Post Office. The former massive, three-story brick structure featured a four-story bell tower and served the city of Asheville from 1892 until 1930. In the years prior to that, the site had been a hog wallow fed by a nearby spring. It was used by hog drovers traveling the Buncombe Turnpike, a seventy-five-mile, gravel and wood plank toll road leading from South Carolina to Tennessee and passing through Asheville. An 1849 journal entry from one traveler declared that he spent the night in an Asheville inn with seventy-five people and 5,000 hogs.

24. Miles Building

1901, remodeled 1925
Haywood Street and Battery Park Avenue
Richard Sharpe Smith, original architect

In 1901 a group of distinguished Asheville civic, business, and political leaders belonging to the twenty-year-old Asheville Club decided to build a new meeting place in the downtown district. The Coxe family owned much of the land in that area, as well as the 1886 Battery Park Hotel, so Frank Coxe (1839-1903), offered to build the new club across the street from the post office, then located on what is now Pritchard Park.

They approached architect Richard Sharpe Smith, who designed what looked much like a three-story, red brick mansion. The third floor contained six bedrooms, reportedly for any members unable to make their way home late at night. The membership list included scores of prominent local names: Coxe, Rankin, Grove, Battle, Carrier, and more.

In 1919 Herbert Miles, an Asheville businessman, purchased the property from the Coxe family. Miles undertook a five-year renovation which by 1925 had transformed it into an office and retail building since known as the Miles Building. It remained in the Miles family until it was sold in 2005, but still remains an office and retail building.

25. F. W. Woolworth Building

1938

25 Haywood Street   Henry Gaines, architect

This fabulous building opened for business in 1938, the same year that Thomas Wolfe died, but is worth the time to step into — and back into time. Designed by Asheville architect Henry Gaines (1900-1986), later one of the founders of Six Associates, it is yet another excellent example of how well Art Deco styling could be adapted for a commercial building in Asheville.

The original soda counter provided tourists and local business-people with a fast and convenient place to have lunch. In the 1960's it was the scene of sit-in demonstrations demanding equal rights for all races. The store closed its doors in 1993, but was purchased in 2000, at which time extensive renovations began. A few years later a working replica of the store's soda fountain reopened, with stylistic touches from the 1950s, and still remains in business. The store has since been renamed Woolworth Walk, reflective of the fact that it currently offers art and quality crafts for sale from more than 150 artisans.

Fitzgerald and Wolfe:

Asheville's Downtown Hotels

Three blocks north of the F. W. Woolworth Building stand two former downtown hotels frequented by both F. Scott Fitzgerald and Thomas Wolfe. They can best be seen from the corner of Haywood Street and Vanderbilt Place next to Pack Memorial Library. Both were competed in 1924, during the height of Asheville's post-war building frenzy, to compete with the Grove Park Inn for the growing number of tourists and traveling salesmen pouring into the city. Of the two, only the Battery Park Hotel looks much the same as it did when completed.

26. George Vanderbilt Hotel
(Vanderbilt Apartments)

75 Haywood Street   William Lee Stoddart, architect   1924

Like the Battery Park Hotel to the west, the George Vanderbilt Hotel was also designed by the same acclaimed New York architect. William Lee Stoddart (1868-1940) had recently moved to Atlanta to begin specializing in Southern hotels intended to serve traveling salesmen. His first commission in Asheville, however, was the 1923 Bon Marche department store, which, ironically, was transformed into a hotel in 1985. He spent much of 1923 in Asheville working on his two downtown hotel commissions. It was also in Asheville that Stoddard met and married his second wife, Sabra Ballinger.

The nine-story hotel, known today as Vanderbilt Apartments for seniors, differed significantly when it opened. Prior to an insensitive 'demodeling' required by the United States government in 1969 to qualify as government subsidized public housing, Stoddard's design included three towers atop the hotel with an open rooftop plaza, as well as extensive detailing around several floor-to-ceiling arched windows across the front. Every shred of architectural detail was either stripped off or covered up in order to

Vanderbilt Hotel.   (North Carolina Collection, Pack Memorial Library, Asheville.)

prove "that public funds were not lavishly spent on public housing projects." In return, downtown Asheville was presented with a bland block of bricks.

In 1935, however, the George Vanderbilt Hotel featured a popular restaurant, bar, and ballroom, as well as shops located on the lower level and accessed from the inclined sidewalk running alongside the building. One of these was the Intimate Bookshop, owned by author Tony Buttitta, who wrote *After the Good Gay Times: Summer of '35, A Season with F. Scott Fitzgerald.*

One night in June of 1935 Scott Fitzgerald stumbled into the Intimate Bookshop beneath the George Vanderbilt Hotel searching for a restroom. He and Buttitta met and eventually began a conversation about books and contemporary authors, including Faulkner, Hemingway, and, of course, Fitzgerald. Throughout the summer of 1935, Scott spent time in the bookstore with Tony, as well as in the Vanderbilt Hotel's bar and ballroom. That August, in a failed attempt to hide from the husband of a young woman he had been having an affair with at the Grove Park Inn, Scott checked into the Vanderbilt Hotel under the name "Francis Key."

27. Battery Park Hotel
(Battery Park Apartments)

1924   1 Battle Square
William Lee Stoddart, architect   Edwin Wiley Grove, original owner

Standing on a slight rise in Asheville's northern downtown district is the red brick, fourteen-story Battery Park Hotel, which was built in 1924 by Edwin Wiley Grove (1850-1927), owner of the historic Grove Park Inn and a noted real estate investor and developer. It is the second hotel by that name to stand on this site and both F. Scott Fitzgerald and Thomas Wolfe spent several nights here during their final trips to Asheville.

The original Battery Park Hotel opened to great fanfare in 1886, six years after the arrival of the railroad set Asheville on its path toward becoming a popular tourist destination. Seeing the town's need for a quality hotel, by 1886 Colonel Frank Coxe had purchased several acres of land around a prominent hill in what today is downtown Asheville. On the twenty-five-acre site he commissioned Philadelphia architect Edward Hazlehurst to design a modern hotel with every fashionable device, including electric lighting and a hydraulic elevator. The sprawling and towering Victorian hotel with its numerous balconies and open porches had offered guests panoramic views of the Blue Ridge Mountains. Among its early lodgers were President Theodore Roosevelt, members of the Rockefeller family, and George Vanderbilt.

In addition to attracting wealthy tourists, for more than three decades the Battery Park Hotel served as the social center for Asheville residents. The opening of the Grove Park Inn in 1913, however, signaled the end of an era for what people began seeing as an outdated hotel. In 1921, during a bizarre family feud between Edwin Wiley Grove and his son-in-law Frederick Loring Seely, E.W. Grove purchased the Battery Park Hotel. Rather than refurbishing it as first promised, however, Grove shocked everyone in Asheville by suddenly demolishing it in 1922.

In place of the beloved 1886 Battery Park Hotel, E.W. Grove hired New York architect William Lee Stoddart to design a 220-room, fourteen-story, brick hotel intended to serve traveling salesmen and middle-class tourists. It opened in 1924 and ignited a breach of contract lawsuit filed against Grove by Fred Seely, who was leasing the Grove Park Inn from his father-in-law. Before the lawsuit went to trial, however, in 1927 E.W. Grove died in his penthouse suite atop the Battery Park Hotel. The Battery Park Hotel closed in 1972 and has since been converted into senior citizen housing.

In August of 1935, while still attempting to avoid the husband of the woman he had been sleeping with at the Grove Park Inn, Scott Fitzgerald checked into the Battery Park Hotel as "Anthony Blaine," a combination of the names of two of his characters. Tony Buttitta, a young writer who befriended Scott that summer, described it in his book, *After the Good Gay Times: Summer of '35, A Season with F. Scott Fitzgerald.*

"Compared to the Grove Park Inn, the hotel was of the commercial kind, like one of the Statler or Hilton chains. He had a rather small room with English fox hunt prints on the walls and appeared out of place in it."

Battery Park Hotel. (North Carolina Collection, Pack Memorial Library, Asheville.)

"The setting seemed to emphasize his pallor and low spirits; he was drinking and his hands trembled, while his mind raced on turbulently. He was pacing from one window to the other in the small room, his speech and movements flowing in a rhythm that came from long practice dictating to secretaries. I glanced from him to the small room and asked why he was there instead of at the Inn. He said he couldn't go there, at least not for a day or two. It was a question of money and too many memories."

As Tom Wolfe was growing up in Asheville, he would have stood on Haywood Street and stared up at the original, sprawling Battery Park Hotel, imaging the difference between staying in the opulent 1886 hotel rather than his mother's ramshackle boarding house. At the age of two, Tom would have been too young to recall seeing President Teddy Roosevelt emerge from the Battery Park Hotel to give a speech to 10,000 avid supporters, but his political father would no doubt have been present.

What is certain is that Tom would have strolled around downtown Asheville on one of his summer visits while teaching English at New York University from 1924 until the publication of *Look Homeward, Angel* in 1929. The acidic response by the townspeople to their portrayal, however, kept him away until the summer of 1937, when he rented a rustic cabin on the outskirts of Asheville in hopes of completing his third novel. By August, though, he needed to escape the throng of curious townspeople who had been dropping in daily to see him.

Without telling anyone in his family, he slipped out of the cabin and checked into the second Battery Park Hotel, where he had been staying many Saturday nights in order to take a hot bath. In his room he continued working on his short story "The Party at Jack's." He also continued drinking as he lamented what was becoming his lost summer. The more he drank, the more convinced he became that his editor Maxwell Perkins and his publisher Charles Scribner's Sons had not represented him properly. From his room that August he began calling up New York publishing houses and blurting out, "I'm Tom Wolfe. Do you want to publish my books?"

At first, most thought it a prank, but by the end of the year Tom had severed his relationship with his mentor Maxwell Perkins, who had invested nearly a decade in the young author, while also working with Scott Fitzgerald, Ernest Hemingway, and others. That December Tom negotiated a new book contract with Harper and Brothers, where Edward Aswell took on the challenge of editing his massive manuscripts into salable books.

Returning to the Thomas Wolfe Visitor Center

Directions: From the corner of Haywood Street and Vanderbilt Place, walk back down Haywood Street to Walnut Street, which leads east four blocks to Market Street and the Thomas Wolfe Visitor Center.

Walking Time: Approximately twenty minutes.

Asheville's reputation as a unique shopping, dining, and sightseeing destination is no better represented than along Haywood Street, Lexington Avenue, and Broadway, each intersecting with Walnut Street on the way back to the Visitor Center. At the corner of Haywood and Walnut Street awaits Malaprops, one of the most well-known and respected independent bookstores and cafés in the region (see below).

Walnut Street is a reminder that Asheville, despite its extensive development, is a still a mountain city. At the bottom of the incline is Lexington Avenue. Once an open drainage ditch for Pack Square, Lexington Avenue is now home to a wide variety of unique shops. The uphill climb along Walnut Street leads to Broadway, another street with an assortment of eclectic shops. The entire area is worth the time spent exploring the amazing assortment of shops and cafes for which Asheville is well known.

Designed by Richard Sharpe Smith and built in 1915, this building first served as the Elks' lodge, then as the Asheville Hotel. In 1997 Malaprops Bookstore moved into the lower level, while the upper floors were converted into living spaces. The unique second floor balcony offers residents a picturesque view of the active downtown scene.

(North Carolina Collection, Pack Memorial Library, Asheville.)

63.

You Can Come Home Again: 1937

"I am going into the woods for another two or three years. I am going to try to do the best, the most important piece of work I have ever done. I am going to have to do it alone. I am going to lose what little bit of reputation I have gained, to have to hear and know and endure in silence again all of the doubt, the disparagement, the ridicule, the post-mortems that they are so eager to read over you even before you are dead."

– Thomas Wolfe to F. Scott Fitzgerald, 1937

28. The Wolfe Cabin

1924
Azalea Road
Max Whitson, builder

Note: The Wolfe Cabin is owned by the City of Asheville but is not open to the public, as it awaits the formation and implementation of a master plan for its future restoration and utilization. Given its remote location, it is not visible from any nearby public road. Historical and current photographs can be viewed at the website listed here.

Information: ThomasWolfeCabin.com

By 1937 Thomas Wolfe had hoped that the uproar caused by his callous portrayal of more than three hundred Asheville people in *Look Homeward, Angel* would have subsided enough to enable him to return home without any awkward confrontations. Encouraged by his family, Tom left New York by bus on April 29, getting off at the small town of Burnsville, thirty-five miles north of Asheville, where he planned to spend a few days with some of his mother's relatives.

Around 10:30pm on Saturday, May 1, Tom stepped out of the soda shop on Main Street, where he saw two men involved in a fight. One of the men, Philip Ray, pulled a gun and fired several errant shots at the other, missing each time. The fight was broken up and Ray was put in jail. Out of curiosity, the next morning Tom visited Philip Ray. Several days later, long after Tom had left town, Philip Ray again met his adversary in Burnsville. This time he shot and killed the other man.

On May 3, after checking out of the Nu-Wray Inn, Tom boarded the bus for Asheville, then took a cab over to his mother's boarding house at 48 Spruce Street. Within hours of Tom's arrival, the phone in the hallway started ringing, and friendly visitors, autograph seekers, and newspaper reporters began lining up on the front porch of the Old Kentucky Home.

Tom remained at the Old Kentucky Home for twelve days, spending much of his time shaking hands and greeting people who came to see him. Since he never bothered getting a driver's license, Tom took several long walks around Asheville, at least one while being interviewed by a local newspaper reporter. As someone recalled, "He walked in any kind of weather, and he strode along like an elephant, a hulking giant of a man swinging his arms."

The Max Whitson Cabin.   *(Thomas Wolfe Collection, Pack Memorial Library, Asheville.)*

Tom had returned to Asheville hoping to work on his third novel and one of his short stories. Unfortunately, the daily line of visitors prevented him from getting any writing done at the boarding house. Upon hearing this, Max Whitson, a childhood friend and former classmate, offered to rent Tom a log cabin tucked away on nineteen acres of woods six miles southeast of Asheville. Tom accepted and began making plans to return for an indefinite stay starting in July.

Tom arrived back at his apartment in New York City on May 15 and spent the next six weeks sorting through thousands of pages of scrawled manuscripts, hoping to pull together a few short stories to generate some desperately needed cash. By the end of June Tom had begun work on a story entitled "The Party at Jack's," which he planned to bring with him to Asheville to complete that summer. On June 26 he wrote to his brother Fred in Asheville:

"I believe a few weeks out there in the cabin will fix me up again. I am eager – more eager than I ever have been – to work, and I believe I will get a lot of work done out there. But I do know how I feel now; I do know what has happened to me and what I have been through these past seven or eight years; and I do know exactly what I want to do now – which is to get out to my cabin, to get some rest and relaxation, and to work – and I can only earnestly pray that all my friends and members of my family will understand this extremely normal, sensible desire, and help me every way they can."

On Friday morning, July 2, Tom stepped off the Asheville train at the Biltmore Station, two miles south of Pack Square. He first telephoned Max Whitson from the station, asking to meet him at the cabin. He then called his mother, apologizing for not coming directly to the boarding house, but promising to host a family dinner at the cabin that Sunday evening. After loading a waiting taxi with his books, reams of his preferred lined yellow paper, his clothes, and his bedding – his mother claimed she could not spare any from the boarding house – Tom headed off for the cabin which was to be his home for the summer.

Located atop a secluded grassy knoll surrounded by large, leafy oak trees, Whitson's cabin seemed an idyllic writer's retreat. Two wooden gates at the base of the knoll marked the narrow gravel road leading up to the cabin. Completely furnished and six miles distant from Asheville and the family boarding house, Tom was thrilled with it. Whitson introduced him to Ed, a local handyman hired to cook and clean up after him. Ed, however, proved to be unreliable. An alcoholic, he often had difficulty recalling Tom's name, calling him instead "Mr. Fox." Tom eventually fired Ed, replacing him with a more reliable man named William.

The cabin had neither electricity nor a telephone, but Whitson had recently installed indoor plumbing and a wood-burning cook stove, along with an oversized bed and a wind-up Victrola, both of which Tom had requested. A wide front porch, a large river stone fireplace, and a tree house added to the ambiance of the rural retreat. Whitson showed Tom a nearby spring clear enough for bathing, but Tom elected to go to the downtown Battery Park Hotel each Saturday night to bathe.

Despite having avoided the crowded boarding house where members of his family had gathered to await his arrival, word of Tom's visit spread quickly through Asheville. The following Monday the *Asheville Citizen* made it official, even going so far as to inform its readers that the famous author had gone into town on Saturday to buy groceries so that he could "be host at a family dinner at the cabin this evening in celebration of the Fourth of July." The paper went so far as to report that Tom had hired "a Negro man to cook and do the housework."

Tom was quickly and reluctantly pulled into a series

Wolfe in the cabin. (Thomas Wolfe Collection, Pack Memorial Library, Asheville.)

of dinners, talks, informal meetings, and parties which were to continue all summer. One of his first stops was at the home of Dr. H.B. Weaver on Chestnut Street, where Lilian "Tot" Weaver, the doctor's twice-divorced daughter, currently lived. The flirtatious Tot had written Tom even before his arrival in Asheville, toasting *Look Homeward, Angel* as the Great American Novel. Upon entering the house, Tom was introduced to Tot's most recent beau, the heralded Art Deco architect Douglas Ellington, who had designed the First Baptist Church, the City Building, the Asheville High School, and the S&W Cafeteria. As both were smitten by the vivacious Tot, that summer Tom and Ellington became rivals for her affections.

In August, whenever the number of unexpected guests at the cabin overwhelmed him, Tom would catch a ride to the Weaver's home on Chestnut Street, where Tot would hide him in one of their rooms. According to Julia Wolfe, "During the last month Tom was here, he lived over at the Weaver's. They had a nice home, very quiet and Miss Weaver would turn him into that big room where they have a long couch, says 'Go in there now,' and he said he had a headache so much. She'd turn him in there and forbid everybody or anybody from going through that door into the room. She wanted him to rest."

While working at the cabin that July, Tom hired a college student, Martha Wrenshaw, to serve as his typist, personal assistant, and occasional driver, paying her fifteen dollars a week. She typically arrived mid-day, often rousing her employer out of bed, from which time they worked until evening. Sometimes Martha would type his handwritten manuscripts, but Tom also enjoyed dictating his fiction as he strode about the room, gesturing with his hands. Martha remained with him for a month, when she was replaced by Virginia Hulme.

An aspiring seventeen-year-old Asheville writer by the name of Wilma Dykeman asked her friend Martha Wrenshaw to arrange a time when she could visit Tom at the cabin. "I will always remember Tom's eyes and hands," Dykeman later recounted. "When he shook hands with you, you felt your hand sort of disappear in this great grasp. His eyes were so consuming – the solid brown that really sees you."

Tom at work in the cabin.

(Thomas Wolfe Collection, Pack Memorial Library, Asheville.)

On July 17, an Asheville newspaper ran another story on Tom, including a picture of him sitting at a dining room table in the cabin, sleeves rolled up on his suspendered shirt, writing longhand. A carton of Chesterfield cigarettes sat next to a kerosene table lamp. As one biographer noted of the photograph, "There is a bruise over his left eyebrow, and his left eye is black and swollen. His bottom lip is discolored. But his knuckles are unskinned." No explanation was forthcoming.

As the days passed, the number of uninvited guests and dinner invitations continued to grow. The less Tom wrote, the more he drank.

In recalling his time living at the cabin, his mother reported, "Tom didn't keep the cabin locked up, but he had a refrigerator and he kept a supply of groceries [and] beer in that refrigerator. And he'd come into town at night and have dinner, go back out there about one o'clock and he'd find the cabin filled with young people dancing – they had a Victrola out there. They'd dance to this music and they'd stay there all night long. Drink up all his beer, he said, or anything else, and say, 'Oh, we're going to stay and cook breakfast for you.'"

On August 8 a deputy sheriff from Burnsville called upon Tom at the cabin, handing him a subpoena to appear in court on August 16. Although Tom had not been in Burnsville the night of the murder, he was called to recount the shooting he had witnessed between the two men a week earlier on July 2. Tom took the bus to Burnsville on Monday, August 16, and spent the day waiting for the attorneys to select a jury. He again slept at the Nu-Wray Inn.

His testimony proved meaningless, as the prosecution had ample witnesses the night of the actual murder to prove Philip Ray's guilt. As Tom later recounted regarding the other witnesses, the lawyers spent their time "digging up all the sore spots in their past, their periods in the chain-gang, the occasion they carved someone to pieces over another woman, etc. I fared pretty well comparatively." The day after Tom left the courthouse, however, in his closing remarks one of the attorneys "denounced me to the jury at great length, saying that I was the author of *Look Homeward, Angel,* an infamous book full of obscenities that had held my family, my relatives, and my town up to shameful inspection."

As Tom later summarized to a friend, "I wanted to come back; I thought about it for years. But my stay here this summer has really resembled a three-ring circus. I think people have wanted to be and have tried to be most kind, but they wore me to a frazzle."

On Sunday, August 22, Tom enlisted the assistance of his typist Virginia Hulme to pack up his papers and drive him to the Battery Park Hotel. He was done with the cabin and all of the constant interruptions. Sequestered in his hotel room, he stewed about his misspent summer, which had only netted him one short story, "The Party at Jack's."

Instead of starting a new story Tom began drinking even more, working up his courage to make a long-contemplated break from Scribner's. Instead of contacting Perkins, however, Tom began dialing various major publishing houses. His opening line reportedly was, "My name is Wolfe. Would you like to publish me?" That December Tom made the break official, switching to Harper's.

By Thursday, September 2, Tom decided he had enough. He spent the day walking around downtown Asheville, paying a final visit to his mother and brother Frank at the Old Kentucky Home, then catching a ride with sister Mabel out to the cabin where they packed up his belongings before heading to the bus station. As he circled the cabin a final time, Tom may well have neglected to climb back up into the treehouse Max Whitson had built. Years later a new owner confessed to having discovered there a stack of scrawled yellow sheets of paper, the words on which he was unable to decipher, so he burned them.

Later, after returning to New York City, Tom wrote to a friend:

"Anyway, that cabin of mine, with its beautiful hill, which I thought was going to be a haven of peace and rest, was about as restful as a subway at rush hour. I had them all out there, from Bill Cocke to the undertaker. But as for peace and quiet, I've gotten more if I had moved my cot out and parked it in Times Square."

In 1982 the privately-owned cabin and property were designated as a Local Historic Landmark. In 2001 the City of Asheville purchased the Whitson property and cabin, which had been steadily deteriorating. The city first stabilized and secured the cabin, Since then the Planning and Urban Design Department has been working with the Preservation Society of Asheville and Buncombe County to determine the future of the building. Non-original additions to the cabin have been removed and the roof temporarily repaired, but the structure remains in need of an extensive renovation and a clear plan for its use before it can be opened to the public. At the present time it remains closed and inaccessible by visitors. For more information, go to ThomasWolfeCabin.com.

The cabin during the stabilization process. It remains closed to visitors.

29. Riverside Cemetery

1885   53 Birch Street
Charles T. Colyer, landscape architect

A slow drive or leisurely walk along the shaded, winding blacktop roads looping throughout Riverside Cemetery is like taking a trip back through a history of Asheville – or thumbing through the pages of *Look Homeward, Angel*.

Directions from the Thomas Wolfe Visitor Center:

Drive north on North Market Street for 100 yards to Woodfin Street;
Turn left onto Woodfin Street and drive two blocks;
Turn right onto Lexington Avenue;
Continue north as it becomes Broadway Street for .3 mile;
Turn left onto West Chestnut Street and drive .4 mile;
Turn right onto Montford Avenue for just 25 yards;
Turn left onto West Chestnut Street and drive .1 mile;
Turn right onto Pearson Drive and go .2 mile;
Turn left onto Birch Street, which ends at the entrance to Riverside Cemetery in .3 mile.

Driving time: approximately ten minutes.

Distance: less than two miles.

Hours: Riverside Cemetery is open to visitors from 8:00am until 8:00pm from April 1 through October 31 and from 8:00am until 6:00pm from November 1 until March 31. Self-guided tour packets are available online, at the main gates, or in the cemetery office, located on the north side on the main road. The office is open by appointment only from 8:00am until 4:30pm, Monday through Friday. Appointments can be made by calling (828) 350-2066. For additional information, go to Ashevillenc.gov and type in "Riverside Cemetery."

Literature: *Asheville's Riverside Cemetery* by Joshua Darty, Arcadia Publishing: Images of America, 2018.

Simply called the Asheville Cemetery when it opened in 1885, Riverside Cemetery overlooks the French Broad River and now encompasses eighty-seven manicured acres sheltered by mature oak, dogwood, pine, poplar, and ginkgo trees. The original landscape design came from Englishman Charles T. Colyer (1837-1919), who intended the grounds to serve as both a cemetery and a public park. He designed the cemetery with five tiers, each separated by a gravel carriageway, since blacktopped. Once it opened, many caskets in smaller church cemeteries were moved to Riverside Cemetery, explaining why some tombstones date earlier than 1885.

In 1952, after a decade of neglect, the city of Asheville assumed responsibility for the historic cemetery, which currently numbers more than 13,000 burials with an estimated 9,000 tombstones and twelve mausoleums. More than 27,000 visitors tour the cemetery each year, paying their respects at the graves of Thomas Wolfe, author O. Henry, architect Richard Sharpe Smith, photographer George Masa, Governor Zebulon Vance, and many Asheville notables – including a few marble angels. As noted historian Joshua Darty has observed, "Riverside quickly established its reputation as one of the foremost cemeteries in the South, with its magnificent mountain views, carefully planned landscapes, imposing mausoleums, and unique monuments."

The Wolfe Family Plot

Directions: Upon passing through the gates, immediately bear to the right on the main road for one hundred yards, then turn left at the first fork, beside the Von Ruck family mausoleum. Continue fifty yards, then, if driving, park on the left side of the roadway. The Wolfe family plot is twenty yards ahead on the left, but there are no parking spaces in front of the plot.

"When he came to the gate of the cemetery he found it open. He went in quickly and walked swiftly up the winding road that curved around the crest of the hill. The grasses were dry and sere; a wilted wreath of laurel lay upon a grave. As he approached the family plot, his pulse quickened a little." – Look Homeward, Angel

The large Wolfe family plot, shaded by two towering oak trees and a delicate dogwood, lies on the western face of the highest knoll in the cemetery. W.O. and Julia Wolfe purchased this plot on October 19, 1918, the day after 26-year-old Benjamin Wolfe died during the deadly

Spanish flu epidemic sweeping across the country. Three other members of the Wolfe family who had been buried elsewhere then had their coffins exhumed and reburied in the family plot: Cynthia Hill Wolfe (1842-1884), Leslie E. Wolfe (1885-1886), and Grover Cleveland Wolfe (1892-1904).

Family members are listed in the order in which they are arranged in the front and back rows in the Wolfe family plot. Fictitious names assigned to them by Thomas Wolfe are italicized.

The Wolfe family plot: Mabel, W,O. Julia, and Tom.

Thomas Clayton Wolfe

Youngest son of W.O. and Julia Wolfe.
October 3, 1900 – September 15, 1938
(Eugene Gant)

No single event in Thomas Wolfe's brief life has been analyzed, discussed, and debated more than his death. Unlike F. Scott Fitzgerald, who died instantly of a heart attack on December 21, 1940, Tom's final days stretched from July 10, 1938, when he came down with a severe cold in Seattle, until September 15, when he died in a Baltimore hospital. Over the course of those two months newspapers across the country ran stories detailing his latest condition for their readers.

After contracting a cold on a trip to Seattle, Tom's condition worsened as it rapidly developed into pneumonia. When a persistent cough released dormant tuberculosis lesions in his right lung, the doctors recommended that the family transfer Tom to Johns Hopkins Hospital in Baltimore. His sister Mabel traveled to Seattle to assess her brother's condition, which soon included severe headaches, confusion, sensitivity to light, soaring temperatures, vomiting, and disorientation.

On Tuesday, September 6, Tom and Mabel began an arduous four-day train ride to Baltimore, pausing in Chicago where Julia Wolfe, much to Tom's dismay, joined them from Asheville. As soon as Tom was admitted to Johns Hopkins Hospital, he was seen by Dr. Walter E. Dandy, considered the premier neurosurgeon in the country. Dr. Dandy, who had never heard of Thomas Wolfe, but whose wife knew about *Look Homeward, Angel,* immediately began preparations to bore a small hole in Tom's head to relieve the pressure caused by an accumulation of fluid. Tuberculosis cells found in the fluid, which reportedly squirted three feet in the air, prompted Dr. Dandy to diagnose "a cerebellar tubercle."

On Monday, September 12, Dr. Dandy removed the top of Tom's skull, where he discovered "myriads of tubercles" attached throughout the brain tissue, concluding in his notes, "Obviously there was nothing that could be done."

For the next three days Tom drifted in and out of semi-consciousness, talking incoherently, vomiting, and having difficulty breathing. His nurse suctioned as much mucus as possible from his throat, but early on Thursday morning, September 15, Tom began desperately gasping for air. He died ten minutes later at 5:30am. Julia, Mabel, and Fred were unable to get from their rooms in time to be present.

Angered that the nurse had not called her in time, Julia Wolfe refused to allow the hospital staff to perform an autopsy on Tom, leaving the actual cause of death open to interpretation. The official death certificate listed it as "tuberculosis meningitis." In reality Tom, like his brother Ben, actually drowned from advanced pneumonia, as the infected air sacs in his lungs filled with fluid until he could no longer breathe.

Tom's funeral was held in the First Presbyterian Church, where he had attended services as a child and regularly walked past it on his way to the North State Fitting School. A decade earlier Tom had described Ben's funeral in words which also described his own:

"The women filled the house with their moaning. Eliza [Julia] wept almost constantly; Helen [Mabel] by fits, in loose hysterical collapse. And all the other women wept with gusto, comforting Eliza and her daughter, falling into one another's arms, wailing with keen hunger. And the men stood sadly about, dressed in their good clothes, wondering when it would be over.

The procession moved off briskly to the smooth trotting pull of the velvet rumps. The mourning women peered out of the closed carriages at the gaping town. They wept behind their heavy veils, and looked to see if the town was watching."

One historian reported that "Mabel, the sibling whom Wolfe was the closest to after the passing of Ben, could not bring herself to attend the [cemetery] service, turning around her car and speeding away as soon as she saw the open grave."

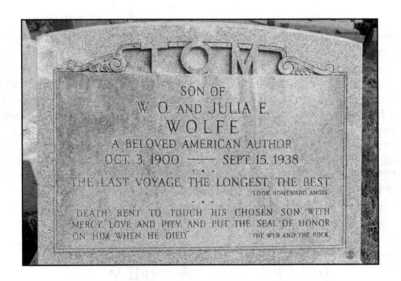

According to an account written nine years later, the cemetery sexton recalled "the gigantic casket they had put into the earth, so huge the removal of a tree had been necessary." Tom's tombstone, which was selected and the inscriptions determined by Julia Wolfe and her children, proudly proclaimed at the top: "Son of W.O. and Julia E. Wolfe" as well as "A Beloved American Author." For whatever reason, neither Tom's middle name Clayton nor its initial appears on his tombstone, a break from Wolfe tradition. A permanent vase in front of his tombstone is generally filled with pens deposited by admirers.

Tom's only two editors, Maxwell Perkins at Scribner's and Edward Aswell at Harper's, were asked by the Wolfe family to each select a quote from his works to be chiseled into his tombstone. Maxwell Perkins selected one from *Look Homeward, Angel*, the novel he had edited: "The last voyage, the longest, the best."

Edward Aswell picked a more recent line, this one from *The Web and the Rock*, which Aswell was then editing and which was released one year after Tom's death: "Death bent to touch his chosen son with mercy, love and pity, and put the seal of honor on him when he died."

William Oliver Wolfe

Father of Thomas Clayton Wolfe.
April 10, 1851 – June 20, 1922
(Oliver Gant)

A towering giant, W.O. was self-taught, but well-read, bombastic, and charming, when he was sober. At the time he met 21-year-old Julia Westall around 1881, he was thirty and already had a dubious record. His first marriage had quickly ended in divorce, he left Raleigh after a scandalous affair and various legal troubles, his second wife Cynthia Hill had just died from tuberculosis, he was a binge drinker, and his new tombstone business was struggling. Their marriage was stormy, to say the least. It effectively ended in 1906 when Julia bought and moved into the boarding house at 48 Spruce Street. His drinking worsened and his work suffered. In 1914 W.O. was diagnosed with prostate cancer. Unable to work, in 1917 he moved into the boarding house. Mabel returned to Asheville to care for their father until his death in 1922 in the Old Kentucky Home. His tombstone proudly proclaims: "Born At Gettysburg, PA."

Julia Elizabeth Westall Wolfe

Mother of Thomas Clayton Wolfe.
February 16, 1860 – December 7, 1945
(Eliza Pentland Gant)

Born into an established, hard-working, but often poor Asheville family, Julia Westall was proud, independent, and self-reliant. Before marrying W.O. Wolfe in 1885, she had been a school teacher, as well as a door-to-door book seller, which is how she came to know the widower in 1884. They shared a love for books and were married a few months later. Julia was willing to move into her husband's home at 92 Woodfin Street, even though it was still decorated with the deceased Cynthia Wolfe's furnishings. A confirmed teetotaler, Julia grew ashamed of her husband's public displays of intoxication. She directed her attention to their children, of whom she bore eight in their first fifteen years of marriage, as well as to her boarding house and her real estate investments.

Julia managed the Old Kentucky Home boarding house she purchased in 1906 the rest of her life. Like so many others in Asheville who had speculated on commercial real estate during the 1920s, she lost all of her investments during the Great Depression, and barely held onto the boarding house. She passed away at the age of eighty-five while traveling in New York City. Near the base of the tombstone she shares with her husband is the following: "Mother Of Five Sons And Three Daughters."

"Gant looked appreciatively at her trim erect figure, noting her milky white skin, her black-brown eyes with their quaint child's stare, and her jet black hair drawn back tightly from her high white forehead. She had a curious trick of pursing her lips reflectively before she spoke; she liked to take her time and came to the point after interminable divagations down all the lane-ends of memory and overtone, feasting upon the golden pageant of all she had ever said, done, felt, thought, seen, or replied, with egocentric delight." – Look Homeward, Angel.

Mabel Elizabeth Wolfe Wheaton

Youngest daughter of W.O. and Julia Wolfe.
September 25, 1890 – September 29, 1958
(Helen Gant)

Ralph Harris Wheaton
Husband of Mabel Wolfe.
December 25, 1881 – June 15, 1973
(Hugh T. Barton)

At age sixteen Mabel took charge of the Wolfe family home at 92 Wood-fin Street when her mother and six-year-old Tom moved into the Spruce Street boarding house. Julia Wolfe had trouble keeping her staff, so Mabel was often called over to help, especially when the boarding house neared its capacity of nineteen guests, all of whom also had to be fed each day. Later Mabel utilized her singing ability to escape Asheville, performing with a friend, Pearl Shope, on the vaudeville circuit for nearly three years before marrying Ralph Wheaton, a salesman. The couple moved back to Asheville when her father grew too ill to work. She cared for him at the boarding house until he died in 1922 from prostate cancer.

Mabel's tombstone includes a line from a letter written by Tom Wolfe on January 29, 1925: "She has more human greatness in her than any woman I've ever known." At the base of the tombstone is a line from *Look Homeward, Angel:* "O lost, and by the wind grieved. Ghost, come back again."

Fred William Wolfe

Second oldest son of W.O. and Julia Wolfe.
July 15, 1894 – April 8, 1980
(Luke Gant)

Mary Burriss Wolfe
Wife of Fred Wolfe.
April 15, 1916 – June 20, 1974

Fred, who was six years older than Tom, proved to be his mentor and protector. A natural salesman, Fred recruited Tom and his friends to sell weekly copies of the *Saturday Evening Post*. Under Fred's guidance Tom also became one of the best newspaper carriers for the daily *Asheville Citizen*.

"He was Luke, the unique. Luke the incomparable: he was, in spite of his garrulous and fidgeting nervousness, and intensely likable person – and he really had in him a bottomless well of affection. He wanted bounteous praise for his acts, but he had a deep genuine kindliness and tenderness." – Look Homeward, Angel

Fred eventually settled in Spartanburg, SC, but remained associated with the Thomas Wolfe Memorial Association he helped found in 1949. He worked closely with the association and the city of Asheville to protect and preserve his brother's legacy until his death in 1980.

Fred is buried with his wife, Mary Burriss Wolfe, who had died six years earlier. On their shared tombstone Fred included: "In Memory Of My Beloved Wife, Mary." Fred proudly had placed beneath his name: "Luke of *Look Homeward, Angel.*"

Cynthia C. Hill Wolfe

William Oliver Wolfe's second wife.
September 18, 1842 – February 22, 1884
(Cynthia Gant, Lydia Gant)

In 1880, after his first marriage ended with a divorce, 27-year-old William Oliver Wolfe married 38-year-old Cynthia C. Hill in Raleigh. Often described as 'sickly,' Cynthia made her living selling women's hats. W.O. decided they should move to Asheville in hopes of improving her health.

The Wolfe family plot is the third place in which Cynthia was buried. After her death on February 22, 1884, W.O. had been given permission to bury Cynthia in the Methodist cemetery. Shortly thereafter another individual came forward claiming to own the same plot where Cynthia had been buried. Angered, W.O. hired three men to dig up her coffin, place it in a wagon, and drive Cynthia to the small Newton Academy Cemetery less than a mile away on Biltmore Avenue.

Two of Cynthia's friends, Julia Westall, soon to become Julia Wolfe, and a Mrs. Bunn, accompanied the casket. According to Julia, "Mrs. Bunn got up on that wagon and made those men open that casket and open the lid and let her look in. She said, 'Oh, that red hair has filled the casket!' Cynthia had red hair – Mr. Wolfe used to call her Reddy. But the brown silk dress she'd been buried in was just like it was."

Cynthia remained at the Newton Academy Cemetery, resting in peace, from March of 1884 until the fall of 1918 when Julia and W.O. Wolfe purchased a large plot in Riverside Cemetery after the death of their son Ben. Despite the fact that W.O. Wolfe had been married to Julia for thirty-three years, he insisted on having Cynthia's coffin unearthed for the third time and reburied in the rear of the new Wolfe family plot.

Frank Cecil Wolfe

Oldest son of W.O. and Julia Wolfe.
November 25, 1888 – November 7, 1956
(Steve Gant)

Already eighteen when in 1906 the Wolfe family was divided between two houses, Frank traveled extensively, changing jobs often and relying on both his parents for money when his latest scheme failed. No one in the Wolfe family seemed to like Frank, whom Tom berated for his foul breath, rotten teeth, "unclean yellow hands, and the clammy and unhealthy sweat that stank with nicotine." Frank seemed to have inherited his father's worst traits, including drunkenness and debauchery.

As adults, Tom never forgot nor forgave Frank for how he had treated him and the rest of the Wolfe family. In turn Frank never forgot nor forgave Tom for how he had been portrayed in *Look Homeward, Angel*. At Tom's funeral Fred Wolfe bluntly stated that Tom would never have wanted Frank to be there.

Grover Cleveland Wolfe

Twin brother of Benjamin Harrison Wolfe.
October 27, 1892 – November 16, 1904
(Grover C. Gant)

In 1904 Julia packed up the younger Wolfe children and took a train to St. Louis, where she rented a large house for the summer and began taking in boarders attending the World's Fair. Tragically, twelve-year old Grover, Ben's twin, contracted typhoid fever and died there. Julia brought the body back to be buried in Asheville's Newton Academy Cemetery before being reburied in Riverside Cemetery in 1918.

In September of 1918 the Wolfe family gathered at the original Woodfin house. Shown left to right are Tom, then a junior at the University of North Carolina, mother Julia, father W.O., brother Frank, his wife Margaret, sister Effie and her children, brother Fred, sister Mabel, and brother Ben, who died just a month after this picture was taken. (Thomas Wolfe Collection, Pack Memorial Library, Asheville.)

Benjamin Harrison Wolfe

Twin brother of Grover Cleveland Wolfe.
October 27, 1892 – October 18, 1918
(Ben H. Gant)

Like his twin brother, Ben was named by his father after one of the 1892 presidential candidates. Ben struggled in school, dropping out after the ninth grade to go to work for an Asheville newspaper. He often protected his younger brother Tom from the family discord, preferring to take neither side, instead openly showing his disgust for both his father and his mother. In 1918 Ben developed symptoms of tuberculosis, most likely contracted from one of the nefarious boarders his mother refused to turn away. When he attempted to enlist in the military that September, the doctors rejected Ben for service, citing "weak lungs."

In October, 26-year-old Ben, his lungs already compromised, was struck down by the flu epidemic. The mutated virus proved resistant to all available medicines. Within two hours of showing classic flu symptoms, the patient's lungs would begin filling with fluid from hemorrhaging tissues, until the patient literally drowned to death. Tom was called home from the University of North Carolina at Chapel Hill, arriving in time to sit at his bedside and talk with his favorite sibling as Ben slowly died.

Tom remarked in a letter he later wrote to his sister Mabel, "I think the Asheville I knew died for me when Ben died. Ben was one of those fine people who want the best and highest out of life, and who get nothing — who die unknown and unsuccessful."

Cemetery historian Joshua Darty reports in his book *Asheville's Riverside Cemetery* that "W.O. [or an employee] carved a small marker for [Ben's] grave to match that of his deceased twin, Grover."

Leslie E. Wolfe

The first child of W.O. and Julia Wolfe.
October 18, 1885 – July 14, 1886

Born nine months after her parents' marriage, Leslie Wolfe lived just nine months before succumbing to cholera. Julia Wolfe always maintained Leslie had died from drinking tainted milk from a neighbor's cow. Leslie was first interred in the Newton Academy Cemetery before being moved to Riverside Cemetery after October of 1918.

Effie Nelson Wolfe Gambrell

Oldest daughter of W.O. and Julia Wolfe.
June 7, 1887 – November 11, 1950
Silver Brook Cemetery, Anderson, SC.
(Daisy Gant)

In 1908 quiet Effie married Fred Gambrell and moved to South Carolina, where they raised their children. Reflective of her attitude toward all of the Wolfe family drama, Effie elected not to live in Asheville nor to be buried in Riverside Cemetery. Instead, she and her husband were buried in the Silver Brook Cemetery in Anderson, SC.

Other Tombstones of Interest

As Asheville's primary cemetery for more than a century, Riverside Cemetery bears the tombstones of scores of individuals of local, regional, and national importance, as well as a few marble angels. Joshua Darty, cemetery director, has compiled a map and list of significant individuals in the region's history who are interred in the cemetery. In addition, he and others painstakingly compiled a list of approximately 150 individuals who are buried in Riverside Cemetery who are also characters in *Look Homeward, Angel,* along with their fictional names and cemetery locations.

The 1913 Sarah Buchanan Angel

For decades people have walked Riverside Cemetery in search of the angel which once stood on the porch of W.O. Wolfe's tombstone shop. The marble angel inspired Thomas Wolfe to take the title of his first novel from "Lycidas," a poetic elegy written by John Milton in 1637 mourning the drowning of a young man at sea.

> *"Look homeward Angel now, and melt with ruth;*
> *And, O ye dolphins, waft the hapless youth."*

An elderly cemetery sexton spoke years after the novelist's death about Tom Wolfe's visits to the grave of his beloved brother Ben. "He was a big man," the sexton went on meditatively, "A giant. I used to see him.

Every time he came to the cemetery, he went to see the angel." As the author of the sexton's story added, "Eagerly I inquired regarding the whereabouts of the angel, and he consented to show us the way. He had a fund of mortuary anecdotes. He showed us an angel, and when we were ready to go I slipped a dollar into his hand."

When the same author relayed this account to Julia Wolfe in 1947, she scoffed: "Why, there's no such thing! That angel he showed you is not the one Tom wrote about. Tom's angel isn't in the cemetery. That man – I've spoken to him about it – he imposes on visitors. He shows them that old angel and tells them that's the one, and then they give him money for tips." When pressed, she said she considered the actual marble angel to be in Hendersonville.

Historians now agree that while there are several tombstones

The Sarah Buchanan Angel (1913).
(*Thomas Wolfe Collection, Pack Mem. Library, Asheville.*)

in Riverside Cemetery which W.O. Wolfe carved and occasionally signed "W.O. Wolfe / Asheville, N.C.," the famed marble angel described by his son in *Look Homeward, Angel* is not in Riverside Cemetery. As Julia Wolfe surmised, the one which comes the closest is the marble angel marking a grave in the Oakdale Cemetery in Hendersonville, twenty-six miles south of Asheville (see entry).

The angel which the sexton enjoyed showing curious tourists stands over the grave of Sarah Elizabeth Buchanan, who died on December 27, 1913, at the age of eighty-three. The largest of any tombstone in Riverside Cemetery, it is prominently positioned in the northwest quadrant overlooking the French Broad River, directly beside one of the black-top roads. While Tom Wolfe may well have studied it, this angel differs significantly from the descriptions he included in *Look Homeward, Angel*:

"For six years it had stood on the porch, weathering, in all the wind and the rain. It was now brown and fly-specked. But it had come from Carrara in Italy, and it held

a stone lily delicately in one hand. The other hand was lifted in benediction, it was poised clumsily upon the ball of one phthisic foot, and its stupid white face wore a smile of soft stone idiocy."

In contrast, the Sarah Buchanan angel is holding a wreath in her left hand rather than a lily, has her right hand clutched to her throat rather than reaching to the heavens, and is looking downward in deep sorrow rather than "with a smile of soft stone idiocy."

The origin of the 1913 Sarah Buchanan angel remains shrouded in mystery. It was not, as many have assumed, carved by Frederick B. Miles (1860-1921) from marble remaining after the construction of the Biltmore House. Miles, an Englishman, arrived in Asheville in 1891 to work for George Vanderbilt, but had moved to Atlanta by 1899.

The Sarah Buchanan angel could possibly have been the work of stonemason Samuel Isaac Bean (1867-1947), who also had come to Asheville to work on George Vanderbilt's mansion. No records have survived, however, to indicate that Samuel Bean either carved or sold angels as large as the Buchanan angel.

What has not yet been ruled out or proven is that the 1913 Sarah Buchanan angel may well have been purchased from W.O. Wolfe. While Wolfe was considered a skilled craftsman, he never received the training necessary to be able to carve a detailed, intricate, life-size angel from an enormous block of imported marble. Historian Ted Mitchel estimated that between 1905 and 1915 W.O. Wolfe sold approximately fifteen imported Italian marble angels from his tombstone shop on Pack Square.

The 1900 Ella McElveen Angel

Thirty yards east of the towering Buchanan Angel is the McElveen mausoleum, topped with a petite marble angel purchased from and installed by W.O. Wolfe. The mausoleum was erected in 1900 by Atlanta businessman George Wyche McElveen for his first wife, Ella Pace McElveen (1859-1900) who died at age forty-one. In 1902 Joseph McElveen, brother of George McElveen, was also laid to rest inside the mausoleum, along with Ella Pace McElveen's mother Parolee Pace (1836-1921).

Although the female figure does not have the traditional wings of an angel, she is considered one of W.O. Wolfe's angels imported from Carrara, Italy. She, too, differs from the description found on the pages of *Look Homeward, Angel*.

Both photos are courtesy of the Thomas Wolfe Collection, Pack Memorial Library, Asheville, NC.

Ella McElveen Angel (1900).   *Lucy Ann Cliff Angel (1914).*

The 1914 Lucy Ann Cliff Angel

Located on a rather steep hillside on the lower southwest quadrant, the marble statue of an angel standing over the grave of Lucy Ann Cliff (1837-1914) also came from the tombstone shop of W.O. Wolfe. An Asheville newspaper article in 1936 mistakenly identified the Lucy Ann Cliff angel as the one which inspired Tom Wolfe, but the author himself repudiated that claim. In addition, the Cliff angel does not fit the description found in *Look Homeward, Angel*, although it is a beautiful work of art and well worth admiring.

Lucy Ann Bannister was born in Leeds, England, and married Dr. Charles Cliff (1830-1911). When Dr. Cliff died in 1911, he was buried in the churchyard cemetery of the Methodist Church in Black Mountain where they lived. Surprisingly, his grave is marked by a small, undecorated tombstone with crudely chiseled letters: "Dr. Charles Cliff 1911." In contrast, when Lucy died three years later at age seventy-seven, her three sons had her interred in Riverside Cemetery under a far more expensive tombstone, complete with an elaborate, imported marble angel embracing a draped cross. Expertly chiseled by W.O. Wolfe on her stone foundation is: "Earth Counts a Mortal Less, Heaven an Angel More." Two of her three sons, as well as other family members, are buried nearby, while Dr. Cliff remains in Black Mountain.

O. Henry
William Sydney Porter

1862-1910
Husband of Sara Coleman Porter.
1868-1959

The 1910 gravesite of famed short story writer William Sydney Porter, also known as O. Henry, is located one hundred yards west of where Thomas Wolfe was buried in 1938.

Directions, Walking: From the Wolfe family plot follow either entrance to the circular blacktop road leading west. Step off the blacktop onto an older, once-graveled, grassy path located between the gravestones for the Tomberlin family on the left and the Artus family on the right. Continue walking west until reaching a set of concrete steps leading down to the Porter family plot on the left. The author's grave is located below the large Smith family tombstone.

William Sydney Porter.

North Carolina Collection, Pack Memorial Library, Asheville.

Directions, Driving: Turn right from the parking area adjacent to the north side of the Wolfe family plot onto the next roadway, then make an immediate left turn. Continue west until reaching the mausoleum for Jill Su on the left, turning left at that curve. There will be an "O. Henry" arrow sign at that point and another closer to his gravesite. Park on the graveled right shoulder of the roadway across from the Shuford-Moore family plot, as there are no parking spaces directly in front of the Porter family area. Walk one hundred yards south on the blacktop road until reaching a set of concrete steps on the left, leading up to the Porter family plot on the right.

Like F. Scott Fitzgerald and Thomas Wolfe, author William Sydney Porter had a difficult time writing in Asheville. The prolific and popular short story writer lived most of his life in New York City, where he became known for his wit, his surprise endings, and his heavy drinking. Among his most memorable stories are "The Gift of the Magi" and "The Ransom of Red Chief." He only lived the final few months of his life in Asheville but is buried in Riverside Cemetery.

Although trained as a pharmacist, as a young man William Porter worked in a Texas bank while attempting to establish his career as a short story writer. He apparently fell prey to sloppy bookkeeping, for he was later convicted of embezzling a missing $854.08 from a bank in Austin. "I took the job and held a position of trust," he explained. "Since I did not report the shortages as they occurred, I can legally be held as an accessory to the fact."

Sentenced to five years in prison, he continued to submit his short stories to major magazines, changing his name to O. Henry to avoid detection by his publishers as a convicted felon. Released after three years for good behavior, the prolific Porter went on to pen a weekly short story for the *New York World* magazine, continuing to use the by-lines Oliver Henry or O. Henry.

After the death of his first wife from tuberculosis, Porter renewed a childhood friendship with Sara "Sallie" Coleman while visiting North Carolina, where he hoped the mountain air would improve his failing health. Their friendship kindled a romance and on November 27, 1907, Sara and William were married and settled in New York City. Early in 1910, as his health declined, the couple moved to Weaverville, just north of Asheville, where Sara had previously lived.

After living for years in chaotic New York City, Porter found it difficult to write in rural Weaverville, so he rented an office in downtown Asheville. As one historian noted, "He missed the hustle and bustle of New York and the inspiration that it gave him. He moved his office to downtown Asheville to be near city life but still found it to be too quiet and not enough people." William also encouraged Sara to become a professional writer, which she did under the pen name of Sara Lindsey.

By this time in his life, however, the effects of his heavy drinking combined with his general poor health had taken a serious toll on the author. "I know I smoke too much," he told his doctor, "keep late hours, and drink too much, but that's about all."

On June 5, 1910, at the age of forty-eight, William Sydney Porter died of heart disease and cirrhosis of the liver. After his death, Sara selected a modest stone with no indication that William Porter was also the author O. Henry. When the Asheville Cemetery Company erected a sign directing curious fans of O. Henry to the gravesite of William Porter, Sara objected, insisting that it be taken down. The cemetery staff removed it upon her request, only to reinstall it after each of her visits. Sara and his daughter from his first marriage were also buried near him.

William Porter left behind a legacy of more than four hundred short stories. Hardback collections of his stories by far outsold those by both F. Scott Fitzgerald and Thomas Wolfe. Years later the city of Asheville recognized William Porter by naming O. Henry Avenue in his honor.

Fans of William Sydney Porter have for decades left pennies atop his gravestone in Riverside Cemetery. Originally they were to total $1.87, an amount inspired by the opening paragraph of "The Gift of the Magi" –

"One dollar and eighty-seven cents. That was all. And sixty cents of it was in pennies. Pennies saved one and two at a time by bulldozing the grocer and the vegetable man and the butcher until one's cheeks burned with the silent imputation of parsimony that such close dealing implied. Three times Della counted it. One dollar and eighty-seven cents. And the next day would be Christmas."

The cemetery staff periodically collects the coins from atop William Porter's tombstone and donates the money to local libraries.

Other Area Notables

The list of individuals buried at Riverside Cemetery who played major roles in Asheville's history, as well as approximately 150 individuals from whom Tom Wolfe drew his inspiration for *Look Homeward, Angel,* is too long to include here. Many can be located using the cemetery map or Joshua Darty's book *Asheville's Riverside Cemetery.*

Among them are the following:

Dr. Samuel Westray Battle (1854-1927)
Thomas Clingman (1812-1897)
Locke Craig (1860-1924)
Isaac Dickson (1839-1919)
Stephen Lee (1801-1879)
Solomon Lipinsky (1856-1925)
William H. Lord (1866-1933)
George Masa (1881-1933)
James Merrimon (1842-1900)
T.S. Morrison (1852-1926)
Thomas Patton (1841-1907)
Richard Pearson (1852-1923)
Jeter C. Pritchard (1857-1921)
William Randolph (1854-1935)
James Rankin (1846-1928)
Richard Sharpe Smith (1852-1924)
Dr. Rodney Swope (1851-1917)
Zebulon B. Vance (1830-1894)
Dr. Carl Von Ruck (1849-1918)
Nicholas Woodfin (1810-1876)

F. Scott Fitzgerald:
His Retreat to North Carolina

30. The Grove Park Inn

1913
290 Macon Ave
Frederick L. Seely and G.W. McKibbin, architects

By the spring of 1935 F. Scott Fitzgerald's life was in shambles. His 1934 novel *Tender Is the Night*, finally completed nine years after the disappointment of *The Great Gatsby*, failed to impress critics or inspire readers burdened by the Great Depression. For the past five years Zelda had been in a series of private mental institutions, which, along with boarding school costs for their teenage daughter Scottie, had drained away all of the money he had earned writing short stories.

By his own estimate, Scott was $40,000 in debt, having for years borrowed money from his agent Harold Ober, his editor Maxwell Perkins, his publisher, and various sympathetic friends.

Scott, c.1937.　　(*Courtesy of and © Princeton University Library.*)

By age 39 Scott, once a Princeton athlete, was a flabby alcoholic and an emotional wreck. His life was made even more complicated by a reoccurring pattern of messy, guilt-ridden affairs. Living in a rented apartment near Baltimore's Sheppard-Pratt Hospital, where Zelda was being treated for schizophrenia, that fall Scott suffered a severe bout of the flu, worsened by his excessive drinking and poor eating habits. Convinced he had contracted tuberculosis, Scott decided to travel south to recuperate.

North Carolina and Asheville were not totally unfamiliar to Scott, who had included a brief reference to the city in his 1920 short story "The Ice Palace." Five years later Jay Gatsby mentions "the sporting life at Asheville and Hot Springs and Palm Beach." In 1937 the Grove Park Inn was the only resort hotel in Asheville which still catered to the rich and famous, including President Franklin D. Roosevelt that September. To survive the Great Depression, however, the owners of the Grove Park Inn also courted traveling salesmen, business conventions, and weddings.

Grove Park Inn, West Side, c.1913   *(Courtesy Omni Grove Park Inn.)*

Financed by pharmaceutical industrialist and real estate developer Edwin Wiley Grove, the Grove Park Inn was designed, constructed, and first managed by his son-in-law Frederick Loring Seely. It opened on July 12, 1913, and began attracting wealthy businessmen from Chicago and New York to Miami Beach and New Orleans to a "big home where every modern convenience could be had, but with all the old-fashioned qualities of genuineness with no sham . . . all attempt at the bizarre, the tawdry and flashily foolish omitted."

"We are three and a half miles from the railroad. The street cars are not allowed to come near enough to be heard. Automobiles are not allowed near the building during the night. Thus we have no smoke, no dust, no train noise. We have pure air, common sense, digestible food, quiet in the bedrooms at night, the finest orchestra outside of New York and Boston, a great organ, and an atmosphere where refined people and busy business men with their families find great comfort and a good time."
– Frederick L. Seely, 1920 brochure

Under Seely's management, the Grove Park Inn earned a stellar reputation for catering to the needs and whims of wealthy entrepreneurs, politicians, entertainers, and industrialists. Included on the guest registry were such familiar names as Henry Ford, Thomas Edison, Harvey Firestone, Harry Houdini, Eleanor Roosevelt, Franklin Roosevelt, Herbert Hoover, Calvin Coolidge, William Jennings Bryan, and scores more. Rooms were furnished in the popular Arts and Crafts style, and the outdoor terraces ringing the hotel were lined with oak rocking chairs for guests basking in the panoramic views of the Blue Ridge Mountains.

A small orchestra played regularly in the Great Hall (above), where silent movies, after being approved by Fred Seely, were shown on a screen over one of the two massive fireplaces. Elevators were nestled inside the fireplaces to silence the sound of the machinery. Fresh seafood was shipped daily from the Carolina coast. Dairy products were trucked from the Biltmore Estate. Waiters wore black jackets and white gloves. Coins were washed nightly and only crisp new bills were handed out by the staff.

While Asheville's own prohibition law prevented the hotel from selling liquor, the staff could legally serve alcohol brought by their guests and occasionally arranged for discreet evening deliveries by local moonshiners. Downstairs a forty-foot swimming pool, beauty parlor, barber shop, pharmacy, game room, billiard table, pool table, and a three-lane bowling alley were available. Trails for hiking and horseback riding had been cut through the surrounding woods. Two outdoor tennis courts were built below the Sunset Terrace and guests enjoyed privileges at the adjacent Asheville Country Club and its famed Donald Ross golf course. Automobile tours around the area were readily arranged. As it soon became apparent, Fred Seely's strict but effective hotel policies, which even discouraged people from bringing children and "dogs of any size, value, color or ugliness," proved successful in attracting the wealthy, appreciative clientele he had targeted "who want to rest and recreate."

E.W. Grove and Fred Seely were also careful not to let "the finest resort hotel in the world" become a haven for tubercular patients. Their general manager and staff were instructed to screen potential guests diligently, so that, in Grove's own words, "no sick people would ever be taken." A staunch and outspoken opponent of unregulated boarding houses, E.W. Grove purchased and leveled a number of boarding houses near his real estate developments on the estimated 1,200 acres of land he owned around Asheville. Even after the 150-room hotel passed out of the control of the Grove and Seely families after 1928, the new owners continued to strictly enforce the prudent policy.

1935: F. Scott Fitzgerald's Arrival

On his first trip to North Carolina in 1935 F. Scott Fitzgerald by-passed Asheville and the Grove Park Inn, electing instead to stay that February in Tryon, forty-five miles to the south. He checked into the modest Oak Hall Hotel, not far from where his friends Nora and Lefty Flynn lived on a small horse farm outside Tryon (see entry).

Failing to find the inspiration in Tryon he so desperately needed to churn out more of his once-popular short stories, Scott soon returned to Baltimore, where his health continued to deteriorate. He checked into Johns Hopkins Hospital, where x-rays revealed that "much more extensive involvement of the lungs has taken place since the previous examination of June 26, 1933. Large areas of infiltration are seen in the right, middle and upper lobes." The examination report did not mention any tuberculous cells. Rather than attributing his lung damage to twenty years of heavy smoking, Scott announced to his friends that he, like his favorite poet John Keats, had been diagnosed with tuberculosis. His Baltimore doctors recommended an extended period of rest, so Scott began making plans to travel to Asheville to meet with Dr. Paul Ringer, a highly respected pulmonary physician.

Arriving alone on May 16, Scott had his choice of several lodging options, ranging from inexpensive boarding houses, including Julia Wolfe's Old Kentucky Home, to the downtown Battery Park Hotel or the George Vanderbilt Hotel, both modestly priced to attract salesmen traveling through Asheville. Instead, Scott felt secure enough in his ability to resume writing short stories for the *Saturday Evening Post* to take a taxi up Macon Avenue to the famed Grove Park Inn resort hotel. There he took rooms 441 and 443 overlooking the front entrance, where from his large open window he could watch guests arrive.

"I hear it is beautiful here," a lonely Scott wrote soon after he arrived, "but without people all places are the same to me."

As he intended, Scott scheduled an examination by Dr. Ringer, who diagnosed his new patient as suffering from exhaustion, alcoholism, insomnia, and cirrhosis of the liver. He found no evidence of tuberculosis in Scott's lungs. His assessment was shared with Albert Barnett, the Grove Park Inn's general manager, who had worked at the hotel since 1923. Mr. Barnett, in fact, had called Dr. Ringer to confirm that his fourth-floor guest did not have tuberculosis. Barnett in turn reported Dr. Ringer's evaluation to Laura Guthrie, an aspiring writer who befriended Scott that summer and who kept a journal of their activities and conversations.

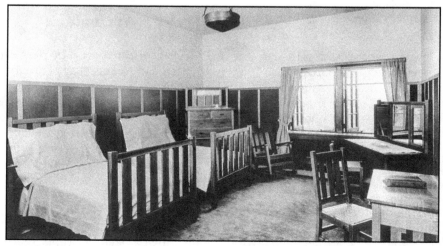

An original guest room, c.1913.   *(Historic photos courtesy of the Omni Grove Park Inn.)*

While Scott desperately needed rest, he also knew that he had to continue writing at the Grove Park Inn. At his request, the hotel staff removed the bed from room 441, replacing it with a couch so that Scott could use that room as his study. A connecting door led to room 443, which remained set up as a bedroom for him. Originally finished with dark oak woodwork, brown burlap wallpaper, and fumed oak Arts and Crafts furniture, by 1935 the guest rooms had been redecorated in more colorful tones. As a visitor to Scott's room described it:

"His back was to me when I entered the brightly lit room of knotty pine and cheer-fully curtained windows. There wasn't a shadow, and the paneling reflected the light like glass. Books, clothes, and papers were scattered about, ash trays piled with butts and bits of rubbish; and there were bottles, all empty but one, which was half-full of gin, and cups, bowls, and an ornate silver coffeepot on a room-service tray precar-iously set near a closet door. The door was ajar; there was a large carton of empty bottles.

Fitzgerald was sitting on the edge of a flower-patterned couch, the tele-phone in one hand, a glass and a cigarette in the other, talking in the same hoarse voice. A dressing gown failed to cover his pale legs, which seemed short for his torso, and his stubby and unattractive feet were showing. When he saw me he fumbled for his slippers and hid his feet in them. Out of cigarettes, he asked if I had any; I shook my head and he dug among the crumpled butts, found a passable one, and lit it."

– After the Good Gay Times

In her 1935 journal, Guthrie recorded that Scott remained se-questered in his room the first few weeks of May, occasionally emerging at night to quietly sit by himself in a corner of the Great Hall, gazing at the young couples dancing to the lively music. Laura earned money to pay for her room in a private home on Macon Avenue by dressing as a gypsy and reading the palms of hotel guests. For the next four months Laura served as Scott's confidant, typist, driver, and friend, for as another acquaintance recalled, "That summer Fitzgerald needed friends to listen to him and to reassure him of his worth." Inspired by Laura's role as a for-tune teller in the Grove Park Inn, Scott sold a short story to the *American Magazine* entitled "Fate In Her Hands."

A little more than a month after his arrival, Scott, who showed little self-discipline when it came to either women or gin, let himself become involved in the messiest of his string of extramarital affairs. A young, attractive, married woman named Beatrice Dance, staying at the Grove Park Inn with her invalid sister, had recognized Scott from his pub-licity photographs. She coyly caught his attention by reading a copy of *The Great Gatsby* in the Great Hall. Beatrice, who came from a wealthy

Tennessee family, soon fell in love with Scott, even offering to leave her husband and daughter for him. Their torrid affair aroused the suspicion of Beatrice's sister, who advised her brother-in-law that he should come to the Grove Park Inn to retrieve them.

Wracked with guilt and distraught with fear of being confronted by her angry husband, Scott fled the Grove Park Inn, making quick trips to Baltimore to see Zelda, to New York for a tryst with yet another of more than fifty women he admitted to having had slept with, to Tryon to see the his friends Nora and Lefty Flynn, and to Lake Lure (see entries).

Upon his return to Asheville, Scott checked into the downtown George Vanderbilt Hotel. Once she found out where he was, Beatrice arranged an ill-advised meeting at the hotel, introducing her husband "Hop" to Scott, claiming they were friends. Hop immediately saw through the ruse, angrily shoving Scott before taking Beatrice back home where she soon suffered a nervous breakdown. Unlike his numerous casual affairs, Scott may well have fallen in love with Beatrice, for they continued to exchange letters, even though they never saw each other again.

After the awkward encounter with Beatrice's husband, Scott again fled to New York, only to return in mid-August to the Grove Park Inn, where the staff reported he consumed several bottles of beer each day. A month later he returned to Dr. Ringer's office, where the doctor recommended that Scott check himself into Mission Hospital to dry out and calm his frazzled nerves. Before leaving Asheville, however, Scott consulted with Dr. Robert S. Carroll, the director of Highland Hospital, located on a prominent ridge less than a mile from the Grove Park Inn, about transferring Zelda to his Asheville sanitarium in 1936.

Discouraged by Zelda's deteriorating condition and wary of Baltimore's approaching winter, Scott retreated south in November of 1935 to the Skyland Hotel, located on Main Street in Hendersonville. More affordable than the Grove Park Inn, Scott arrived there nearly broke, later admitting that he survived at the Skyland Hotel by eating canned meats and washing his clothes in a sink. "It was funny," he added, "coming into the hotel and the very deferential clerk not knowing that I was not only thousands, nay tens of thousands in debt, had less than forty cents cash in the world and probably a thirteen-dollar deficit at my bank."

It was at the Skyland Hotel where Scott wrote his own literary obituary, a three-part confessional entitled "The Crack-Up," which he was able to sell to *Esquire* magazine in three monthly installments beginning in February of 1936. Scott had hoped people would view his emotional collapse of 1935 as a necessary first step toward the revival of his writing career. Instead the consensus among editors and publishers was that Scott was washed-up, unreliable, and out of touch with their readers.

1936: A Year of Despair

Buoyed by the modest payments from *Esquire* and his long-anticipated inheritance after his mother's death, Scott returned to Asheville in April, bringing Zelda with him. After checking back into his familiar rooms 441 and 443 at the Grove Park Inn, Scott drove Zelda to Highland Hospital. In July he traveled over in his "ancient Packard roadster" to pick her up, taking her to a large swimming pool which was then a part of Beaver Lake in north Asheville, not far from Highland Hospital.

Once there, Scott dove from the fifteen-foot high platform, apparently in an attempt to show off his athletic prowess for Zelda. Instead, he hit the water awkwardly, dislocating his shoulder and snapping his collarbone. He then had to spend several weeks in his hotel room encased in a plaster cast around his upper torso. He later described the incident to Beatrice Dance, his former lover, as well as to another friend:

"Did I tell you that I got the broken shoulder from diving from a fifteen-foot board, which would have seemed modest enough in the old days, and the shoulder broke before I hit the water . . . ? I split my shoulder and tore the arm from its moorings, so that the ball of the ball-and-socket joint hung two and one-half inches below the socket joint.

"When it was almost well, I tripped over the raised platform of the bathroom at four o'clock one morning when I was still surrounded by an extraordinary plaster cast and I lay on the floor for forty-five minutes before I could crawl to the telephone and get rescued. It was a hot night, and I was soaking wet in the cast, so I caught cold on the floor of the bathroom, and a form of arthritis called 'myotosis' developed, which involved all of the joints on that side of the body, so back to the bed I went, and I have been cursing and groaning without cessation until about three days ago, when the devil began to abandon me.

"To make a long story short, I was on my back for ten weeks, with whole days in which I was out of bed trying to write or dictate, and then a return to the impotency of the trouble: the more I worried, the less I could write.

"During this time Mother died in the North and a dozen other things seemed to have happened at once, so that it will take me several months to clear the wreckage of a completely wasted summer, productive of one mediocre short story."

That September, living in fear of being forgotten and desperate for publicity, Scott agreed to an interview with Michael Mok, a writer for the *New York Post*. Unfortunately, what Scott had envisioned as his literary rebirth materialized as his literary obituary. Entitled "The Other Side of Paradise, Scott Fitzgerald, 40, Engulfed in Despair," the article was published on September 25, the day after his birthday. In part it read:

"The poet-prophet of the post-war neurotics observed his 40th birthday yesterday in his bedroom of the Grove Park Inn here. He spent the day as he spends all his days - trying to come back from the other side of paradise, the hell of despondency in which he has writhed for the last couple of years.

He had no company except his soft spoken, Southern, maternal and indulgent nurse and this reporter. With the girl he bantered in conventional nurse-and-patient fashion. With his visitor he chatted bravely, as an actor, consumed with fear that his name will never be in lights again, discusses his next starring role. He kidded no one. There obviously was as little hope in his heart as there was sunshine in the dripping skies, covered with clouds that veiled the view of Sunset Mountain.

Physically he was suffering the aftermath of an accident eight weeks ago, when he broke his right shoulder in a dive from a fifteen-foot springboard. But whatever pain the fracture might still cause him, it did not account for his jittery jumping off and onto his bed, his restless pacing, his trembling hands, his twitching face with its pitiful expression of a cruelly beaten child.

Nor could it be held responsible for his frequent trips to a highboy, in a drawer of which lay a bottle. Each time he poured a drink into the measuring glass on his bedside table, he would look appealingly at the nurse and ask, "Just one ounce?"

Yesterday, toward the end of a long, rambling, disjointed talk, he put it in different words: 'A writer like me,' he said, 'must have an utter confidence, an utter faith in his star. It's an almost mystical feeling, a feeling of nothing-can-happen-to-me, nothing-can-harm-me, nothing-can-touch-me. Thomas Wolfe has it. Ernest Hemingway has it. I once had it. But through a series of blows, many of them my own fault, something happened to that sense of immunity and I lost my grip.'"

Discovering that the damaging *Post* article was being read, discussed, and lamented by all of his New York friends, editors, and publishers, Scott panicked. He reached for the phial of morphine pills his doctor had prescribed to ease the pain of his broken collarbone, swallowing all that remained. When his nurse arrived, she discovered Scott passed out on the bathroom floor, where he had thrown up enough of the morphine to survive his suicide attempt.

After his diving accident, in addition to a hired nurse, Scott also required the services of a secretary who could type his dictated stories and letters for him. In 1936 Asheville resident Martha Marie Shank served as Scott's stenographer for a short while. Thirteen years later, when a biographer asked about reports of Scott's attempted suicide at the Grove Park Inn, she wrote:

"You may or may not know that while he was here he made two attempts at suicide. One was before I knew him. He had taken something and was found lying on the bathroom floor. This information is from Dorothy [Richardson, his nurse].

The second one occurred while I was seeing him, though I was not there at the time. He called and asked me to come out and when I got there he asked Dorothy and me to be seated. This was unusual. Then he sat down, looking serious, and said, 'Dorothy, tell Martha Marie what I did.'

Dorothy was angry and said, 'All right, I'll tell her. Scott tried to kill himself.' (She seemed to take it as a personal affront.) She then went on to tell me the details of his getting his pistol and threatening to shoot himself. There was quite a commotion. In some way she got a bellboy, who got the pistol, and Scott, in pajamas and bathrobe, chased him over the hotel.

After that, the hotel refused to let him stay there by himself. If Dorothy went out, I had to be there. Dorothy thought he was serious in the attempt. While she was telling me the story, he listened with all the interest of never having heard about it before. But he had little if any comment to make."

While a small hole in the ceiling of room 441 is occasionally attributed to Scott's pistol, no one associated with him at that time reported a gun going off in his room. As his secretary also recalled:

"The stenographic work I went to the Inn to do soon amounted to little or nothing – he wrote only the most necessary business letters and a very few personal ones, the latter being chiefly to Scottie. But he liked to have us there . . . . Sometimes he was gay and talkative and utterly charming. At others he was tragically depressed. Meals were sent up to his rooms and Dorothy and I did our level best to get him to eat, but I never saw him take more than a few bites. Apparently, he lived on gin and beer – that is what he drank all the time I was there. I have no idea how much gin he averaged a day, but it was plenty."

By this time the general manager and staff at the Grove Park Inn had grown weary of Scott's behavior, including his complaints about being denied all the alcohol he had ordered, and were threatening to make him leave. After taking Zelda to see a Saturday afternoon football game with Nora and Lefty Flynn in October, Scott started making plans to return to the Oak Hall Hotel in Tryon.

In December of 1936 F. Scott Fitzgerald checked out of the Grove Park Inn for the final time, but left Zelda under the care of Dr. Carroll at Highland Hospital. After spending Christmas with Scottie in Baltimore, Scott returned to North Carolina, living from January through June at the Oak Hall Hotel in Tryon. Realizing his career as a short story writer was over, Scott finally quit drinking, hoping that he could provide for Zelda and Scottie by convincing the movie producers at M-G-M to hire him as a screenwriter. One afternoon that May, while still living in the Oak Hall Hotel, Scott entertained Thomas Wolfe and his family.

The call from Hollywood came in July of 1937. Scott took the train to California, where he met and soon moved in with Sheila Graham, a celebrity newspaper columnist. His $1000-a-week salary enabled him to begin paying off some of his debts, but his inability to produce the style of writing his directors required cost him his job in 1938.

Zelda and Scott. (Courtesy of and © Princeton University Library.)

Convinced he still had one more novel in him, Scott began writing *The Last Tycoon*. Two years later, with his novel nearly complete, Scott suffered a fatal heart attack in Sheila Graham's apartment, where he died December 21, 1940. He was forty-four years old. The unfinished novel was published by Scribner's the following year.

For additional information on F. Scott Fitzgerald's time in western North Carolina, please see the sections on Hendersonville, Tryon, and Lake Lure, as well as Tony Buttitta's book, After the Good Gay Times.

Zelda Sayre Fitzgerald
Asheville: 1936 - 1948

31. Highland Hospital

Established 1912
19 Zillicoa Street
Dr. Robert Carroll, original owner

In the spring of 1936 Zelda Fitzgerald began her twelve-year association with Highland Hospital, which ended with her death there on March 10, 1948. Dr. Robert Carroll had established the infamous mental institution in 1912 on a landscaped fifteen-acre campus. It included several buildings which still stand, including Homewood, his former residence. The site of the wooden hospital building where Zelda and eight others perished in a deadly fire has since remained a grassy knoll. A plaque honoring Zelda is located in the front lawn of nearby Highland Hall. It contains her quote:

"I don't need anything except hope, which I can't find by looking backwards or forwards, so I suppose the thing is to shut my eyes."

Directions from the Thomas Wolfe Visitor Center:

Drive north on North Market Street one block to Woodfin Street;
Turn left onto Woodfin Street and drive two blocks;
Turn right onto Lexington Avenue;
Continue north as it becomes Broadway for .3 mile;
Turn left onto West Chestnut Street and drive .4 mile;
Turn right onto Montford Avenue and drive one mile;
Turn right onto Zillicoa Street.

Distance: less than three miles.
Driving time: approximately 10-15 minutes.

In 1904 Dr. Robert Carroll founded a small, downtown mental health facility first known as "Dr. Carroll's Sanatorium." Five years later he moved several blocks north to a picturesque ridge at the end of Montford Avenue overlooking the French Broad River. In 1912, after creating an idyllic, fifteen-acre landscaped campus, which included his residence "Homewood," he renamed it Highland Hospital. As its reputation grew, Highland Hospital received applications from across the country, but Dr. Carroll typically restricted the number of his patients to sixty-five.

In contrast to more typical mental hospitals of the era, some of which were simply insane asylums with notorious padded cells and straitjackets, Dr. Carroll advocated carefully monitored diets, handicrafts, team sports, gardening, occupational training, and outdoor exercise, including a daily vigorous five-mile hike. He banned outside drugs, alcohol, and tobacco, and restricted their intake of sweets, replacing them with fresh vegetables, milk, eggs, and fruit juice.

Dr. Carroll and his staff, however, also experimented with more alarming forms of treatment which most modern physicians have since classified as harmful, sometimes even inhumane, as they often destroyed their patients' mental capacity. Zelda Fitzgerald was one of his patients who on numerous occasions was subjected to insulin shock therapy.

In 1939 Dr. Carroll transferred ownership of Highland Hospital to Duke University, where it became part of their Neuropsychiatric Department. Under their agreement, Dr. Carroll remained as the medical director until his official retirement on January 1, 1945.

After the Highland campus was no longer utilized as a hospital, the buildings and property were sold individually in 1990. They have each since served a variety of functions and have at times sat vacant. The three central remaining structures are:

Homewood – Looking much like a medieval castle, this granite structure served as Dr. Carroll's home. His wife, Grace Potter Carroll, was an accomplished pianist and gave performances and music lessons in their home. One of her many students was vocalist and songwriter Nina Simone. After the Carroll's moved, the home became a dormitory for nurses. It has most recently been used as a venue for special events and offices.

Rumbough House – In 1892 Montford Mayor James E. Rumbough built this beautiful, 9,000-square-foot Queen Ann home, which features inlaid flooring, leaded stained-glass windows, wrap-around porches, tiled fireplaces, and handcrafted woodwork. After purchasing it in 1912, Dr. Carroll utilized the building as the Administrative Building for Highland Hospital. It was later used as a diagnostic laboratory.

Highland Hall – Easily identified by its colonial white columns, this four-story, red brick building was constructed by Dr. Carroll to serve his growing number of patients. A granite marker and plaque dedicated to Zelda Fitzgerald were placed on the front lawn featuring the quote from a letter she had written to Scott. Below is the former structure where Zelda was housed and where she perished.

Highland Hospital.   *(North Carolina Collection, Pack Memorial Library, Asheville.)*

Zelda's Breakdown

As it now seems painfully clear, the April 3, 1920, marriage of Zelda Sayre, the impetuous belle of Montgomery, to Francis Scott Fitzgerald, the 24-year-old best selling author, was doomed from the very beginning. As they soon demonstrated, both Scott and Zelda were persistently tormented by insecurity, jealousy, and guilt. Neither could manage money, alcohol, or parenthood, and they each needed what the other proved incapable of providing: a strong mate to guide them through the turbulent waters of their nomadic, creative, and chaotic lives.

The first strains appeared after the 1922 publication of Scott's second novel, *The Beautiful and the Damned*, when Zelda accused him of plagiarizing passages from her missing diary. To retaliate Zelda declared she too would become a professional writer, and together they began to weave a sticky web of jealousy, anger, deceit, resentment, and bitterness.

"I lived in a quiet, ghostly, hypersensitive world of my own," she later recalled. "Scott drank."

To smooth over the roughness in their marriage, they both soon drank to excess, steadily transforming themselves from being the life of any party to becoming a pair of rude, boorish, and nasty drunks. As a close friend recalled, "The aftermath of a Fitzgerald evening was notoriously a painful experience." In the end, they both lost their battle for top billing.

Zelda was the first to crack. In 1924 they were living in the south of France where Scott was working on his final draft of *The Great Gatsby*. Bored, Zelda became involved with a handsome, young French aviator she met on the beach. After being confronted by Scott, she attempted suicide by swallowing several sleeping pills. A few years later, although already twenty-seven years old and still intent on writing for the magazines, Zelda became intoxicated by the consuming desire to become a professional ballet dancer.

"I went into dancing because I was miserable in my personal life, and I thought I could dance," she wrote. "That was a delusion." Fatigue soon led to anxiety, which then led to depression. In 1930, while still living in Europe, she and Scott agreed she should enter a Swiss sanitarium, where she was diagnosed and treated as schizophrenic.

"I was completely insane," she later confessed.

In 1930 Scott was still attempting to write a sequel to *The Great Gatsby*, which had received positive critical reviews in 1925, but failed to generate sustained sales. He began drowning himself in alcohol and self-pity, blaming Zelda's mental breakdown for his literary impotence. At the same time, he also began to realize that the carefree, yet chaotic lifestyle he had fostered was contributing to Zelda's collapse. As noted biographer Nancy Milford summarized, "What Zelda needed was peace, calm, and reassurance of herself at every point of uncertainty. Scott could not give what he did not have."

After a year of treatment in Switzerland, Zelda was released. Within a year, however, Zelda suffered a major relapse and in 1932 she entered the Henry Phipps Psychiatric Clinic of Johns Hopkins University Hospital. In 1934 she was transferred to nearby Sheppard-Pratt Hospital.

As part of her therapy, the doctors encouraged Zelda to resume her writing. In a matter of an amazing few weeks she completed an autobiographical novel entitled *Save Me the Waltz*, which she sent to Scott's editor, Maxwell Perkins, at Scribner's. Scott, who had set aside the pages of his novel to churn out mindless, but profitable short stories to pay for her treatment, was understandably livid, as Zelda's plot mimicked Scott's unfinished manuscript for *Tender Is the Night*. When released by Scribner's, neither of their novels sold well, leaving both Scott and Zelda blaming the other for their failure as writers, parents, and partners.

Zelda's Arrival in Asheville

"I think about Zelda, those days when I was in love with a dazzling light, I thought she was a goddess. Triumphant, proud, fearless. Going at top speed in the gayest worlds we could find. She reached and took all the things life put before her, until she collapsed and could reach no more. Now she's a pathetic figure who reads her Bible. Broken, humiliated, her radiant eyes with no luster, her fiery hair a frazzled mop."
– Scott Fitzgerald, 1935

In the spring of 1936, after he had spent most of the previous year in North Carolina, Scott decided Zelda needed a change in both her environment and her treatment. It may well have been Dr. Paul Ringer, Scott's Asheville physician, who suggested Highland Hospital.

Insulin Shock Therapy

As innovative as Dr. Carroll was, not all of his methods of treating mental disorders would meet with approval today. As one historian noted, "Not only was he instrumental in the 'groundbreaking' introduction of electroshock therapy as a means of curing mental illness, but was also a proponent of the use of insulin injections and shots of horse blood administered directly to the spinal column." As one of Dr. Carroll's brochures openly declared:

"It is gratifying to note the increased percentage of recoveries from mental disorders which result from insulin, drug, and electric shock and sub-shock treatments, reinforced by modern occupational and re-educational therapy. The hospital staff includes physicians whose training in therapeutic shock represents years of experience in both Europe and America. Cases of mental depression, hypochondriasis, the early stages of schizophrenia, confused states, and defective volition are amenable to treatment."

First developed in 1927, insulin shock therapy was administered to patients, such as Zelda Fitzgerald, who were suffering from schizophrenia and who were not responding to standard treatments. For the next thirty years it was promoted as a highly successful form of treatment in psychiatric hospitals across the United States. In the 1950s, however, further evaluation revealed that insulin shock therapy was no more effective than other less dangerous forms of treatment.

In the laborious procedure, the patients were injected with a massive overdose of an insulin hormone strong enough to send them into a coma. The patients first experienced violent seizures, including thrashing, moaning, groaning, and rolling in their beds, as the staff attempted to restrain them. Eventually each patient would slip into a coma, generally allowed to last an hour, before the staff administered glucose to reverse the body's violent reaction to the overdose of insulin hormone.

This extreme procedure was typically repeated six days a week for two months at a time. There were no established guidelines, so doctors and their staffs often experimented with stronger doses and extended periods of treatment, in one instance for two years. After each treatment the insulin patients had to be carefully monitored by the hospital staff, as delayed convulsions from the induced coma were always a threat, so the patients were often housed together.

The theory behind the insulin injections and induced coma was that the treatment would literally 'shock' the patients out of their mental illness, restoring the brain's nerve cells to their normal function. In truth, the treatment often caused irreversible brain damage, which was interpreted as a positive result, since the patients no longer experienced fear and anxiety. The treatments also conveniently made difficult patients easier for the staff to handle. Morality rates, when reported, ran as high as five percent. One survivor of fifty insulin-induced comas described the treatments as "the most devastating, painful, and humiliating experience of my life."

While the precise number of insulin doses administered to Zelda remains unknown, there is no question that she was subjected to numerous insulin shock treatments. Whether or not it can be directly attributed to the treatments, Zelda's condition did gradually improve, at least temporarily. She grew from being totally withdrawn at the beginning of the summer of 1936 to taking part in a New Year's Eve costume ball. A later photograph of the volleyball team shows a defiant Zelda standing in the center of the front row, holding the ball as if to dare anyone to try to wrestle it from her. Dr. Carroll rewarded Zelda for her improvement by giving her permission to walk the campus unsupervised. As one of the staff recalled:

"We were careful with Zelda; we never stirred her up. We tried to get Zelda to see reality; tried to get her to distinguish between her fantasies, illusion and reality. This is not easy for a schizophrenic. The psychotherapy was very superficial. We let her talk out things which bothered her. She often rebelled against the authority, the discipline . . . . She didn't like discipline, but she would fall into it."

Life – and Death – Without Scott

Although Scott was just a few minutes away and owned a 1927 Packard he kept in Asheville, Dr. Carroll and his staff discouraged him from visiting Zelda too often, bluntly stating, "You are her emotional dis-organizer." Scott occasionally grumbled about it to others, declaring, "I have been within a mile and a half of my wife all summer and have seen her about a half-dozen times." When permitted, Scott would generally bring Zelda back to the Grove Park Inn for lunch, which, according to hotel employees, they often ate in silence, while Scott smoked incessantly.

While Scott gallantly kept from Zelda the depths of his financial, emotional, and creative despair, he did inform her that he would be leaving Asheville in July of 1937. After arriving in Hollywood and beginning his short-lived career as a screenwriter, Scott often wrote to Zelda. However, he never mentioned that he was living with the young, attractive Sheila Graham, a vivacious and popular Hollywood socialite who penned a gossipy newspaper column about the movie industry. Those who knew them both often said that Sheila Graham looked like Zelda in the bloom of her youth.

Scott returned East in September and again at Christmas to see both Zelda and sixteen-year-old Scottie, who lived with friends in Connecticut where she attended a private boarding school. These quick visits gave Scott the encouragement to plan a trip for the three of them to Virginia Beach in March of 1938, but the vacation proved a disaster. Zelda was irritable, Scottie was resentful, and Scott was drunk. Afterwards he wrote Dr. Carroll from Hollywood:

"Each time that I see her something happens to me that makes me the worst person for her rather than the best, but a part of me will always pity her with a sort of deep ache that is never absent from my mind for more than a few hours: an ache for the beautiful child that I loved and with whom I was happy as I shall never be again."

The studio executives at M-G-M did not offer to renew Scott's contract for 1939, but he was convinced he had gathered enough material about the movie industry to write another novel. Entitled *The Last Tycoon*, Scott worked on it for two years while still living with Sheila Graham, but he had returned to drinking straight gin and was prone to angry outbursts. In a letter to Scottie he described himself as "depressing, over-nervous about small things, and dogmatic." He was again broke and often sick. He wrote letters to Zelda and Scottie almost weekly, as well as to Dr. Carroll, begging him not to release Zelda prematurely on account of any lapse in his monthly payments. He continued working on his novel, which was more than half complete when Scott suffered a massive heart attack and died in Sheila Graham's apartment on the afternoon of December 21, 1940.

During this time Zelda continued to show improvement at Highland Hospital. Dr. Carroll and the staff began letting her go into Asheville alone. They also asked her to help teach some of the gym classes and for Christmas of 1939 allowed her to travel to Montgomery to visit her mother. Buoyed by these brief tastes of freedom, Zelda worked to convince Dr. Carroll she could be released from the sanitarium. In April of 1940 Zelda was officially discharged and returned to Montgomery. Scott's death in December shocked her, as it did all of his friends who had grown accustomed to hearing of his various illnesses, but who never thought he was ever close to dying. Scott's life insurance policy enabled Zelda to receive an annuity of fifty dollars a month for the rest of her life.

Scottie was married in New York in February of 1943, but Zelda did not feel stable enough to attend. Living with her mother in Montgomery was not easy for Zelda, as she was constantly reminded of her younger days as a Southern belle. She socialized very little, preferring to stay in her room where she continued to write and to paint. In August of that year she returned to Asheville, checking herself back into Highland Hospital for additional insulin injections.

On September 6, 1943, during one of her trips into Asheville, Zelda climbed the steps to the porch of the Old Kentucky Home, just as Scott had done eight years earlier. After meeting Julia Wolfe, Zelda signed the register, paid $3.50 for a week's stay, and moved into her second-floor room. Although one biographer suggested she and Julia Wolfe became friends that week, no evidence points to an extended stay or any return visits by Zelda to the Wolfe boarding house.

In February of 1944 Zelda felt confident enough to return to Montgomery. As one of the hospital staff remarked, "she looked almost pretty again, and cheerful. But, you see, it just wasn't permanent." In Montgomery Zelda again turned to religion as her salvation and escape, primarily remaining in her room and only occasionally speaking with curious visitors. In 1946 she again spent the summer receiving additional treatments at Highland Hospital, but returned to Montgomery for the winter.

On November 2, 1947, Zelda suffered a relapse and returned to Highland Hospital for additional treatments. "She was a chronic schizophrenic — that's what we always understood," offered one of the staff.

108.

"So that would be hard — that she really wasn't going to get better." As was the practice at Highland Hospital, patients who had been given the insulin treatments were assigned one of the rooms on the top floor.

Highland Hospital.   (N.C. Collection, Pack Memorial Library, Asheville.)

On the night of March 10, 1948, a fire started in the basement kitchen of the old structure, which had never been equipped with fire alarms or a sprinkler system. The smoke and flames were immediately drawn up a nearby dumbwaiter shaft which acted as a chimney. As the flames reached each floor, they shot out of the shaft and down the hallways leading to the rooms. The wooden fire escapes soon burnt like kindling under the intense heat. When the firemen arrived, they and the staff struggled to get the women out of the lower floors. On the upper floors they found the doors locked and "heavily screened porches and windows shackled with chains as a precautionary measure to keep patients from jumping out." Forced back by the intense flames, the firemen were unable to rescue Zelda and eight other women who were trapped in their rooms.

Recently the son of one of the patients who escaped the blaze posted his mother's recollection of that fateful night. She, like Zelda, had been assigned a room on the upper floor. Despite having been given a sedative that evening, as was standard practice, his mother had been able to flee down the stairs. The woman helped several other patients escape to the safety of the grounds, where neighbors and staff were gathering, but she failed in three attempts to reach Zelda's room before the firefighters pulled her away. Before they did, her hair had been singed and her nightgown nearly caught on fire. As the Asheville newspaper reported:

"*Fire roared through a mental hospital here early today and snuffed out the lives of nine women patients. They died as twenty others, some screaming, some calm, were led to safety. Flames quickly engulfed the four-story central building of the Highland Hospital for nervous diseases. Wailing of some of the twenty-nine women echoed over the spacious grounds. Firemen, police, nurses, doctors and townspeople rushed to the rescue. But seven women were trapped on the upper floors. Two others removed by firemen died in a short while. It was the third fire in the hospital in less than a year. Fire Chief J. C. Fitzgerald said two broke out last April. One ignited a mattress and the other started from oil-soaked rags tucked under a stairway.*

Chief Fitzgerald said he believed today's fire started in the kitchen of the hospital's central building. But that had not been officially determined. Dr. B.T. Bennett, hospital medical director, estimated the fire loss at $300,000. Miss Betty Uboenga of Lincoln, Ill., assistant supervisor, described how she and Supervisor Frances Render of Scarboro, W. Va., first went after the helpless patients.

'We felt that the others were awake and would help themselves,' she said. 'As soon as we got the helpless ones out and safely put away elsewhere, we rushed back to help others. By then we knew some had been trapped. Some of them were awake, we know, and were rousing the others. It seemed no time at all until the entire building was like a furnace.'"

March 10, 1948.   (*North Carolina Collection, Pack Memorial Library, Asheville.*)

The brilliant four-story blaze on a prominent ridge could be seen from all over Asheville that night, drawing nearly one thousand people to the scene. They, like the staff and firemen, could only stand and stare. A nurse later lamented, "All we could do was watch, hear the screams, and smell the flesh burning."

110.

A Lingering Mystery

An investigation into the fire led Asheville officials to determine that an electric coffee urn in the basement kitchen had malfunctioned, igniting the deadly blaze. Their report concluded by stating that "there was negligence, but not to the extent to be classed as culpable negligence."

At least three other theories have doggedly persisted as to the fire's origin. The easiest to discount is that Zelda set the fire herself. In addition to being the furthest away from the source of the fire, the fact that Zelda died in the fire on the top floor would seem to cast serious doubts on the validity of that theory. The second is that a grease fire in the kitchen quickly spread to the upper floors, but no reports have been found to substantiate that distinct possibility.

Perhaps the most provocative theory about the origin of the fire involves night supervisor Willie Mae Hall. She was one of Dr. Carroll's former patients whom he felt he could safely hire to help supervise his patients. Hall reportedly had set two fires while living in Raleigh prior to coming to Highland Hospital. Many now believe that Willie Mae Hall deliberately set the fire. So far, this theory also remains unsubstantiated.

It has often been stated that Zelda's remains were located the following day by the discovery of her corpse near one of her charred, red ballet slippers. While a dance slipper might have survived the fire, a report from the Morris Funeral Home provides additional information:

"They cannot get the bodies out of the ruins before Friday p.m. Two bodies were removed Thursday night during the fire. They were only identified by jewelry they had on at that time. There is going to be a question on the identities of the remaining seven bodies still in the ruins unless there is jewelry or other means of identification. Received call Mrs. Zelda Fitzgerald's body has been positively identified by dental work. The body will be shipped Sunday, March 14, and arrive at Union Station in Washington at 4:45 p.m. March 15. Due to disfiguration casket cannot be opened."

On March 17, 1948, Zelda was buried beside Scott in the Protestant Rockville Union Cemetery in Rockville, MD. In November of 1975, at their daughter's request, Scott and Zelda were moved without fanfare to the Fitzgerald family plot at St. Mary's Catholic Church Cemetery in Rockville, where they both remain. On their shared tombstone is Scott's final line in *The Great Gatsby*:

"So we beat on, boats against the current, borne back ceaselessly into the past."

Hendersonville:

F. Scott Fitzgerald's Retreat

Thomas Wolfe's Mysterious Marble Angel

Located twenty-six miles south of Asheville, the town of Hendersonville, population 14,000, offers an attractive array of shopping, dining, history, antiques, music, and leisurely living. Both F. Scott Fitzgerald and Thomas Wolfe journeyed to Hendersonville, which is also the site of the most famous of the marble angels which came from the Wolfe tombstone shop, making the town a popular destination for readers of their novels.

Directions to Main Street: F. Scott Fitzgerald and Thomas Wolfe both traveled from Asheville to Hendersonville on Highway 25, which now is lined with more than twenty miles of businesses and stoplights. A faster route today would be along I-26. From Asheville, I-26 can be accessed from either I-40 West or I-240 West at the major interchange a few miles west of Asheville. From I-26 East, exit 49-B leads into Hendersonville via Highway 64 West. After nearly a mile of fast-food restaurants and shopping centers, Highway 64 intersects historic downtown Main Street. At the corner of Highway 64 and Main Street stands the six-story, brick 1929 Skyland Hotel, where Scott Fitzgerald stayed several nights.

Driving Time: 30-40 minutes.

Directions to Oakdale Cemetery: To journey to the site of W.O. Wolfe's most famous marble angel, continue west on Highway 64 past Main Street for an additional mile. The highway bisects Oakdale Cemetery with three options for turning south onto the cemetery's narrow access road: Valley Street, Prince Street, and the cemetery's main entrance. The tall marble angel can be seen on the left from Highway 64 and is located just seventy-five feet south of the historical marker.

The Henderson county seat was organized in 1840 on a rolling mountain plateau traversed by the 1827 Buncombe Turnpike. Traders and travelers headed north from South Carolina toward Tennessee often paused here before climbing toward the Blue Ridge Mountains.

The town's early planners wisely designed a generously wide Main Street running north and south, intending it to serve as both the town's commerce center and as an early attraction for tourists looking to escape the heat and humidity of the deep South. Once the railroad connected Hendersonville to Asheville in 1886, the town's future was assured, as it has since drawn full-time residents and curious visitors, including both Tom Wolfe as a child and F. Scott Fitzgerald, who stayed at the Skyland Hotel on Main Street in 1935.

Left: The Skyland Hotel on Main Street.   *Baker-Barber Collection; Community Foundation of Henderson County; Henderson County Public Library.*

Hendersonville's downtown district, the second largest in western North Carolina, is centered along a six-block stretch of wide sidewalks and free parking spaces dotted with park benches and carefully tended flower gardens. More than one hundred shops and twenty-five restaurants, most locally owned, line the bustling business district. Included are the Henderson County Heritage Museum and the town's Visitor Center, where information is available on the various festivals, street dances, music events, and art, craft, and antiques shows taking place along Main Street, as well as nearby wineries, breweries, and apple orchards.

F. Scott Fitzgerald's Retreat:

32. The Skyland Hotel

1929
538 N. Main Street

Like Asheville, the small town of Hendersonville was swept up and carried forward into the Roaring Twenties by the wave of expansion set off by the end of World War I. Intended to serve both tourists and traveling businessmen, the six-story Skyland Hotel opened on June 29, 1929, just twelve weeks before the disastrous stock market crash. It featured seventy-five rooms for guests, as well as an elegant ballroom, a large balcony off an upper sun room, and space for five businesses around the airy ground floor lobby. In 1947, as the next post-war economy improved, thirty-two additional rooms were added. In 1974, the owners elected to transform the hotel rooms into condominium units, renaming the structure the Skyland Building. The once-spacious Art Deco lobby has since been segmented into commercial spaces.

After his disastrous affair in 1935 at the Grove Park Inn, that fall Scott Fitzgerald returned to his apartment in Baltimore. Discovering that Zelda's mental condition had deteriorated even more while a patient at Sheppard-Pratt Hospital, Scott looked for yet another safe haven. Practically broke, he knew he could not afford to stay in New York City or at the Grove Park Inn. Instead, he elected to check into the Skyland Hotel, located halfway between Asheville and Tryon, the home of his friends Nora and Lefty Flynn. As he described the move a few weeks later:

"One harassed and despairing night I packed a briefcase and went off a thousand miles to think it over. I took a dollar room in a drab little town where I knew no one and sunk all the money I had with me in a stock of potted meat, crackers, and apples. But don't let me suggest that the change from a rather overstuffed world to a comparative asceticism was any Research Magnificent. I only wanted absolute quiet to think out why I had developed a sad attitude towards sadness, a melancholy attitude toward melancholy, and a tragic attitude toward tragedy – why I had become identified with the objects of my horror or compassion.

I had a strong sudden instinct that I must be alone. I didn't want to see any people at all. I had seen so many people all my life. I was an average mixer, but more than average in a tendency to identify myself, my ideas, my destiny with those of all classes that I came in contact with. I was always saving or being saved. I lived in a world of inscrutable hostiles and inalienable friends and supporters.

But now I wanted to be absolutely alone, and so arranged a certain insulation from ordinary cares.

It was not an unhappy time. I went away and there were fewer people. I found I was good-and-tired. I could lie around and was glad to, sleeping or dozing sometimes twenty hours a day and in the intervals trying resolutely not to think."

– "The Crack-Up"

"It was funny," he later recalled, "coming into the hotel and the very deferential clerk not knowing that I was not only thousands, nay tens of thousands in debt, had less than forty cents cash in the world and probably a thirteen-dollar deficit at my bank."

The Skyland Hotel.

Baker-Barber Collection; Community Foundation of Henderson County; Henderson County Public Library.

He then also included the following notation in his journal, most likely after receiving a long-awaited check for one of his short stories:

"Today I am in comparative affluence, but Monday and Tuesday I had two tins of potted meat, three oranges, a box of Uneedas [biscuits], and two cans of beer. When I think of the thousand meals I've sent back untasted in the last two years . . . . It was

fun to be poor, especially if you haven't enough liver power for an appetite. But the air is fine here, and I liked what I had, and there was nothing to do about it anyhow.

The final irony was when a drunk man in the shop where I bought my can of ale said in voice obviously intended for me, 'These city dudes from the East come down here with their millions. Why don't they support us?'"

It was at the Skyland Hotel in late 1935 that Scott composed what he had expected to be his personal and public literary awakening, a three-part series now known as "The Crack-Up." Desperate for money, Scott sold the idea to the editor at *Esquire* magazine, then immediately began begging for an advance on his payment. The first installment appeared in the February issue as a rambling confessional laced with naïve regrets reaching back to when he was a young man "not being big enough (or good enough) to play football in college, and at not getting overseas during the war."

Scott also used the first of the three articles to evaluate where, as a thirty-nine-year-old, former best-selling author, he now stood:

"There is a sort of blow that comes from within — that you don't feel until it's too late to do anything about it, until you realize with finality that in some regard you will never be as good a man again. [This] happens almost without your knowing it but is realized suddenly indeed. I had been only a mediocre caretaker of most of the things left in my hands, even of my talent.

One should be able to see that things are hopeless and yet be determined to make them otherwise. This philosophy fitted on to my early adult life . . . . Life was something you dominated if you were any good. Life yielded easily to intelligence and effort, or to what proportion could be mustered of both. It seemed a romantic business to be a successful literary man . . . . Of course, within the practice of your trade you were forever unsatisfied — but I, for one, would not have chosen any other.

For seventeen years, with a year of deliberate loafing and resting out in the center — things went on like that, with a new chore only a nice prospect for the next day. I was living hard, too. 'Up to forty-nine, it'll be all right,' I said. 'I can count on that. For a man who's lived as I have, that's all you could ask.'

And then, ten years this side of forty-nine, I suddenly realized I had prematurely cracked. Sometimes, though, the cracked plate has to be retained in the pantry, has to be kept in service as a household necessity. It can never again be warmed on the stove nor shuffled with the other plates in the dishpan; it will not be brought out for company, but it will do to hold crackers late at night or to go into the icebox under leftovers . . . ."

Scott originally entitled the second two articles in "The Crack-Up" series as "Pasting It Together" and "Handle with Care." They followed in the

March and April issues of *Esquire* in 1936. After still more confessionals and bouts of self-pity, he began focusing on how he was going to pull his emotional and literary life together to move forward:

"Suffice to say that after about an hour of solitary pillow-hugging, I began to realize that for two years my life had been a drawing on resources that I did not possess, that I had been mortgaging myself physically and spiritually up to the hilt.

The question became one of finding why and where I had changed, where was the leak through which, unknown to myself, my enthusiasm and my vitality had been steadily and prematurely trickling away.

I must continue to be a writer because that was my only way of life, but I would cease any attempts to be a person — to be kind, just, or generous. There was to be no more giving of myself — all giving was to be outlawed henceforth under a new name, and that name was Waste.

The decision made me rather exuberant, like anything that is both real and new. As a sort of beginning there was a whole shaft of letters to be tipped into the wastebasket when I went home, letters that wanted something for nothing — to read this man's manuscript, market this man's poem, speak free on the radio, write notes of introduction, give this interview, help with the plot of this play, with this domestic situation, perform this act of thoughtfulness or charity.

The man I had persistently tried to be became such a burden that I have "cut him loose" with as little compunction as a lady cuts loose a rival on Saturday night.

I have now at last become a writer only."

Scott had naively hoped his friends, editors, and readers would interpret his emotional and public confession as a necessary and noble first step toward the revival of his writing career. Instead, Hemingway mocked him, his editor Maxwell Perkins was embarrassed for him, and his agent Harold Ober felt it signaled the end of his literary career. His former editors and publishers came away feeling Scott was still emotionally bankrupt and just as unreliable as he had recently demonstrated.

Buoyed, though, with the *Esquire* checks in his bank account, in the spring of 1936 Scott checked out of the Skyland Hotel and headed back to his apartment in Baltimore. There he began making arrangements to transfer Zelda to Asheville's Highland Hospital in April and for him to return to the Grove Park Inn.

Thomas Wolfe in Hendersonville

Unfortunately, Hendersonville's charm seemed lost on Thomas Wolfe, who proved no more charitable to Hendersonville than he had been to his family and friends in *Look Homeward, Angel.* In 1913 his father had purchased a five-passenger Ford, prompting Tom to recall in his notorious novel:

"On Sunday they made long tours into the country. Often they drove to Reynoldsville [Hendersonville], twenty-two miles away. It was an ugly little resort, noisy with arriving and departing cars, with a warm stench of oil and gasoline heavy about its broad Main Street. But people were coming and going from several states: Southward they came up from South Carolina and Georgia, cotton-farmers, small tradesmen and their families in battered cars coated with red sandclay dust. They had a heavy afternoon dinner of fried chicken, corn, string-beans, and sliced tomatoes at one of the big boarding-house hotels, spent another hour in a drugstore over a chocolate nut-sundae, watched the summer crowd of fortunate tourists and ripe cooled-skinned virgins flow by the wide sidewalk in thick pullulation, and returned again, after a brief tour of the town, on the winding immediate drop to the hot South."

33. Oakdale Cemetery

Home of Wolfe's Fabled Marble Angel

Prior to the founding of Hendersonville in 1840, early settlers had no option but to bury their deceased in family plots, occasionally in their own back yards. As Hendersonville grew, its civic leaders recognized the need for a municipal cemetery. In 1883 the city council established the Oakdale Cemetery, located one mile west of Main Street on five acres of land.

The council then prohibited residents of Hendersonville from burying anyone outside an established cemetery. In their initial plan for Oakdale Cemetery, African-Americans were to be buried in a small parcel of cemetery land on the north side of Highway 64; white residents were to be buried on a larger section on the south side of the highway. The cemetery was expanded in 1913 and in 1938 land was set aside for a Jewish section of the cemetery. Later purchases expanded cemetery boundaries on both sides of the highway, until today it totals approximately twenty-two acres of land with more than 5,400 interments.

In 1923 and again in 1955, two local congregations were granted permission to move to Oakdale Cemetery earlier burials on land needed for their building expansions. One of the deceased who in 1923 was moved from the Methodist Episcopal churchyard to Oakdale Cemetery was Walter Bryson. When Walter joined the Confederate Army at the outbreak of the Civil War, his father sent George Mills, an eighteen-year-old slave who had grown up alongside Walter, to accompany his son.

Tragically, young Walter Bryson was one of the 22,717 men killed in a single day, September 17, 1862, at the Battle of Antietam, fought near Sharpsburg, Maryland. It ranks as the bloodiest day in American history. In contrast, the total number of American servicemen killed on June 6, 1944, during the invasion of Normandy, was 6,603.

That evening, after General Lee's surviving forces had retreated back into Virginia, George Mills went onto the battlefield to search among the dead and dying for the body of his childhood friend. He brought him back the nearly five hundred miles to Hendersonville, where Walter Bryson was buried in the cemetery of the Methodist Episcopal Church.

George Mills beside the casket of Walter Bryson, 1923. (Baker-Barber Collection; Community Foundation of Henderson County; Henderson County Public Library.)

Sixty-one years later, the casket of Walter Bryson was raised from the churchyard burial ground, transported, and interred in Oakdale Cemetery. It was accompanied by none other than 79-year-old George Mills. Three years later, in 1926, George passed away and was buried in the same cemetery as his childhood friend Walter – across the road in the African-American section.

119.

The Wolfe Angel

Twenty-nine-year-old Thomas Wolfe took the title of his first novel from "Lycidas," a poetic elegy written by John Milton in 1637 mourning the death of a young man who drowned at sea.

> *"Look homeward Angel now, and melt with ruth;*
> *And, O ye dolphins, waft the hapless youth."*

The book's title and Tom's descriptive passages recalling the marble angel which stood outside his father's tombstone shop have inspired many readers to seek out the actual marble statues. While W.O. Wolfe was considered a skilled craftsman, he never received the training necessary to be able to carve a detailed, intricate, life-size angel from an enormous block of marble. In the novel Tom describes his father as a young man named Oliver Gant, seeking to learn a trade:

"When he was still fifteen, he had walked along a street in Baltimore, and seen within a little shop smooth granite slabs of death, carved lambs and cherubim, and an angel poised upon cold phthisic feet, with a smile of soft stone idiocy . . . . As the boy looked at the big angel with the carved stipe of lily stalk, a cold and nameless excitement possessed him. The long fingers of his big hands closed. He felt that he wanted, more than anything in the world, to carve delicately with a chisel. He wanted to wreak something dark and unspeakable in him into cold stone. He wanted to carve an angel's head.

He never found it. He never learned to carve an angel's head. The dove, the lamb, the smooth joined marble hands of death, and letters fair and fine – but not the angel." – Look Homeward, Angel

By 1900, the year of Tom's birth, W.O. Wolfe had his own tombstone shop on the square:

"It was a two-story shack of brick, with wide wooden steps, leading down to the square from a marble porch. Upon this porch, flanking the wooden doors, he placed some marbles; by the door, he put the heavy simpering figure of an angel."
– Look Homeward, Angel

As biographer David H. Donald confirmed, William Oliver Wolfe "made a good enough living from his tombstones so that the Wolfe family was better off than nine out of ten families in Asheville. A skilled craftsman, he lettered inscriptions with precision, and he had a talent for carving little lambs, or hands folded in prayer, on his monuments. Occasionally he sold one of the seven-foot funerary angels, made of Carrara marble, which he had accepted on consignment and displayed on the porch outside his shop."

"No one knew how fond he was of the angel. Publicly he called it his White Elephant. He cursed it and said he had been a fool to order it. For six years it had stood on the porch, weathering, in all the wind and the rain. It was now brown and fly-specked. But it had come from Carrara in Italy, and it held a stone lily delicately in one hand. The other hand was lifted in benediction, it was poised clumsily upon the ball of one phthisic foot, and its stupid white face wore a smile of soft stone idiocy."

– Look Homeward, Angel

Margaret Johnson Angel (1905), Oakdale Cemetery.

Biographer and historian Ted Mitchel estimated that between 1905 and 1915 W.O. Wolfe sold approximately fifteen marble angels from his tombstone shop on Pack Square. Author Bob Terrell found that Wolfe had purchased at least eight of them from a Pennsylvania wholesaler who imported the statues from Italy.

Discovered several centuries ago, the famed white marble of Carrara in the northern Tuscany region has since been sought by sculptors, architects, and builders around the world. Marble from the more than 650 quarries which once operated in the area can be found from Rome's Pantheon to Boston's Harvard Medical School. In 1501 Michelangelo selected the pure white Carrara marble for his towering statue "David."

Wolfe sleuths have located at least six North Carolina angels which may well have been sold by W.O. Wolfe: the Ella McElveen angel and the Lucy Ann Cliff angel in Asheville's Riverside Cemetery; the Hattie Dalton McCanless angel in the Old Fort City Cemetery; the Fannie Everett Clancy angel in the Bryson City Cemetery; the Otelia Davies angel in Waynesville's Green Hill Cemetery; and the Margaret Bates Johnson angel in Hendersonville's Oakdale Cemetery. It still remains to be determined if the Sarah Buchanan angel also in Riverside Cemetery came from Wolfe's shop. The three angels in Riverside Cemetery are discussed in greater detail in this book.

One of the Wolfe angels may have been lost by W.O. in a poker game. Samuel A. "Mac" McCanless (1859-1923), a professional photographer in Asheville and Old Fort, reportedly played poker with W.O. Wolfe. According to McCanless' niece, Samuel's second wife, Geneva, once complained that he must have loved his first wife, Hattie, more than her, as evidenced by the seven-foot marble angel he had bought for Hattie's grave. "I didn't buy that tombstone," he explained in his defense. "I won it in a poker game." He then added, "I used to gamble with old man Wolfe."

The search for the marble angel which had inspired Thomas Wolfe began not long after the 1929 publication of *Look Homeward, Angel*. In an article which appeared in the November 20, 1949, issue of the *Asheville Citizen-Times*, Virginia T. Lathrop noted that the debate had already persisted for two decades. The article applauded the diligence of local historian Myra Champion, who "has followed every clue, talked to every person who might know anything, and run down every possible angel in Western North Carolina. She has established definitely that there was not just one angel which stood on the marble shop porch, but several. And of this collection, only one answers the description given by Thomas Wolfe. That one is in Oakdale Cemetery in Hendersonville, marking the grave of Mrs. Margaret Bates Johnson."

According to family reports, in 1905 the Margaret Johnson angel standing in Oakdale Cemetery was purchased by her sister from W.O. Wolfe. Margaret's husband, the Reverend Harvey F. Johnson, D.D. (1831-1886), had passed away nineteen years earlier in Mississippi. Both Margaret, who also died in Mississippi, and her husband were brought back to Oakdale Cemetery, where many of their ancestors had been buried.

As his own tombstone indicates, Reverend Harvey Johnson had been born in Buncombe County on January 7, 1831, and died at the age of just fifty-five in Brookhaven, Mississippi, on August 4, 1886. He was one of thirteen children, many of whom remained in the Hendersonville area. After graduating from college, Reverend Johnson served as both a chaplain and a soldier in the Confederate army. In 1867 he was named president of Whitworth Female College in Brookhaven, where he was still presiding when he contracted yellow fever and died in 1886. The college historian called him "one of Whitworth College's most influential presidents."

Margaret Bates Johnson was born on May 13, 1832. She appears to have remained in Brookhaven after her husband's death in 1886, as she died there nineteen years later on May 26, 1905, at the age of seventy-three. The quote below the angel reads, "Her children arise up, and call her blessed."

Cemetery historians attribute the chiseled lettering on her tombstone to William Oliver Wolfe. While the base does not bear his name, historians have noted that stonecutters and engravers of the era only occasionally did so. As was documented for the Oakdale Cemetery's application for the National Register for Historic Places:

"W.O. Wolfe, the Asheville marble cutter, who operated a marble works on Pack Square, placed this and other Italian marble angels in front of his shop as advertisement and as crown jewels of the trade that he so regularly admired and aspired to create. The marble angel stands over fifteen feet tall with a lily in her left hand and her right hand is pointing upward. The detailed and precise carving required to produce a large marble angel like Oakdale Cemetery's angel was beyond the grasp of W.O. Wolfe and other marble cutters in North Carolina. The angel is a work of the stonecutting art that very few in the profession were able to master during the time that it was carved. Wolfe sold the monument to Johnson's daughter [or sister] for $1,000 after visiting her and taking with him photographs of some of the grave-markers at his Asheville shop, as well as this angel."

The Oakdale angel has stood relatively unchanged since 1905. As a precaution, however, the angel has since been protected by a wrought iron fence.

The Carl Sandburg Home and Farm

34. Connemara

1839, restored 1945 and 1974
81 Carl Sandburg Lane
1800 Little River Road (GPS address), Flat Rock
Christopher Memminger, original builder

For those with an interest in another American literary figure with a notable North Carolina connection, just four miles south of downtown Hendersonville near the village of Flat Rock is "Connemara," the 246-acre Carl Sandburg Home National Historic Site.

Directions: The scenic four-mile jaunt from downtown Hendersonville to 81 Carl Sandburg Lane in Flat Rock is worth the time. Head south on Highway 25, also known as the Greenville Highway, until reaching Little River Road, near the Flat Rock Playhouse. Turn right on Little River Road, then left onto Carl Sandburg Lane. The parking lot and visitor center are well marked. Wear comfortable shoes as some walking is involved.

Driving Time: Less than fifteen minutes.

Time at the Site: Allow two hours.

The famed American poet, folk singer, songwriter, and historian was born in Galesburg, Illinois, on January 6, 1878, and lived much of his life in the Midwest. In 1945 he and his wife Lilian purchased "Connemara," an 1839 farmhouse and 246 acres of woods and pastures on the slope of Big Grassy Mountain near the village of Flat Rock. They undertook an extensive, two-year remodeling of the rambling, three-story farmhouse, also adding numerous bookshelves for his 12,000-volume research library. In addition to their three children, two of their grandchildren also lived for several years on the farm with Lillian and Carl Sandburg.

His wife Lilian selected Connemara for the peace and solitude Sandburg needed to write, as well as for the pastures, sheds, and barns she wanted for her three breeds of champion dairy goats. The farm also includes several ponds, hiking trails through the woods, an apple orchard, and numerous gardens.

Carl Sandburg lived at Connemara for twenty-two productive years, passing away at the age of eighty-nine on July 22, 1967. During that time he wrote nearly one-third of his published works and was awarded three Pulitzer Prizes, a Grammy Award, and numerous other accolades. Upon his death President Lyndon Johnson proclaimed him "the voice of America."

Carl Sandburg at Connemara.   *(North Carolina Collection, Pack Memorial Library, Asheville.)*

Soon after his death, Lilian elected to sell Connemara to the National Park Service, which undertook an additional restoration of the house and property before opening it to the public in 1974. The restoration preserved the house just as it appeared shortly before Sandburg's death in 1967. The research collection now includes more than 325,000 items, ranging from his books, letters, photographs, and telegrams to his notes, manuscripts, records, and motion picture recordings.

In addition, the National Park Service continues to maintain several goats descended from Lillian Sandburg's original herd. The popular National Historic Site is open daily, except New Year's Day, Thanksgiving, and Christmas, and attracts nearly 90,000 visitors a year. For more information, visit their website www.nps.gov/carl/index.htm.

Tryon:
F. Scott Fitzgerald's First and Final
Trips To North Carolina

For more than a century the village of Tryon, straddling the border between North and South Carolina, has attracted tourists from the north seeking relief from the cold and from the south looking to escape summer's oppressive heat. Most early visitors stayed at the 1882 Oak Hall Hotel and as one historian has noted, "Many who first became acquainted with Tryon while guests at Oak Hall built or bought homes here."

In addition to F. Scott Fitzgerald, the list of notable visitors and residents includes playwright William Gillette, actor David Niven, novelists Margaret Culkin Banning, Margaret Morley, and Ernest Hemingway, composer George Gershwin, First Ladies Grace Coolidge, Lou Hoover, and Eleanor Roosevelt, social workers Jane Addams and Madeline Yale Wynne ("the social lioness of Tryon"), artist David Silvette, artisans Charlotte Yale and Eleanor Vance, and socialites Lady Nancy Astor and Nora and Lefty Flynn.

Directions using Route 25: When both F. Scott Fitzgerald and Thomas Wolfe traveled to Tryon, their only option was to take a slow, but picturesque two-lane state highway. That is still an option today, as Route 25 leads from Asheville through Hendersonville and alongside Flat Rock, where Highway 176 then splits off to the village of Saluda, population 700, before winding its way through and down the mountains to Tryon.

Distance: 45 miles (approximately 80 minutes).

Directions using I-26: A faster route involves taking I-40 West or I-240 West from Asheville to I-26 East, which bypasses Fletcher, Mountain Home, and Hendersonville. The Saluda exit from I-26 East then heads west to Highway 176, the junction of which is eight miles north of Tryon.

Distance: 45 miles (approximately 60 minutes).

35. The Lure of Tryon

Now a charming town of 1,600 people, Tryon was founded as a foothills settlement along an Indian trading path. Nestled amid 3,000-foot peaks, the peaceful village initially attracted those looking to escape the heat and humidity of South Carolina. When in 1877 the Asheville-Spartanburg Railroad completed the final section of tracks through the mountains surrounding the town, people from as far north as Chicago and as far south as Miami began taking one of six daily trains passing through Tryon.

Photographer and author Margaret W. Morley toured Tryon while collecting material for her influential 1913 book *The Carolina Mountains*. In it she dubbed Tryon as "Traumfest," writing:

"Traumfest lies in a nook of the Blue Ridge Mountains . . . Here lingers a touch of summer even in midwinter, because of the evergreen trees and shrubs that so abound. And here spring comes early, for Traumfest lies in the thermal belt, that magic zone where, although it may freeze, there is never any frost."

Trade Street, downtown Tryon, c.1900.

"Strangers say that Traumfest reminds them of an Old World village, with its bright painted houses and the little church with its square stone tower, the gift of one who lived here and loved the place. It adds to the unstudied effect of the place that its houses are set at every angle, each person placing his as fancy dictates, but avoiding as by instinct planting any building square with the points of the compass."

1935: Scott and Scottie Arrive

Desperate for a break from witnessing Zelda's downhill spiral at Shepard-Pratt Hospital in Baltimore, in February of 1935 Scott took thirteen-year-old Scottie out of school and brought her to Tryon, where his friends Nora and Lefty Flynn lived on a small horse farm. Their first stop was the Oak Hall Hotel overlooking Tryon's South Trade Street, where Scott secured a room for them.

Once she discovered that Scott had brought his daughter with him, Nora Flynn rescued Scottie from the hotel, as Scott, fueled daily with several bottles of beer, was struggling to write a story for the *Saturday Evening Post* to generate more badly needed cash. The story proved a failure, but Scott and Scottie enjoyed their time in Tryon and at the Flynn's home. Father and daughter left Tryon three weeks later, but over the course of the next two and a half years Scott returned several times.

Oak Hall Hotel, c. 1940.

On his final trip to Tryon in 1937, Scott stayed at the Oak Hall Hotel from January until early July before moving to Hollywood for the last few years of his life. On May 5 of that year Tom Wolfe, along with his brother, sister, and mother Julia, drove down to Tryon to spend part of the afternoon on the veranda of the Oak Hall Hotel visiting with Scott. It was the final meeting between the two authors. Scott provided drinks for Tom and his brother that afternoon but declined any himself. "I'm off it like a dirty shirt," he declared. "I can't take the stuff." *(See page 140 for details.)*

The Oak Hall Hotel

Constructed in 1882 soon after the completion of the Spartanburg to Asheville railway, what started as a modest wooden structure gradually expanded in proportion to the growing popularity of Tryon. Built on a bluff overlooking the town's commercial Trade Street and the nearby railroad station, by 1912 the three-story Oak Hall Hotel boasted sixty-six guest rooms, wrap-around covered verandas, and a spacious dining room.

Guests could fill their days with hikes, horseback rides, shuffleboard, bowling, and tennis, as well as browsing through the shops stretched along Trade Street. In addition to attracting tourists, the hotel also served as a popular site for wedding receptions, social activities, and special events. Unfortunately, after several unsuccessful attempts to modernize the historic hotel, it was demolished in October of 1979 to make way for a condominium development.

The Notorious Nora Langhorne and Lefty Flynn

In 1910, Maurice "Lefty" Flynn (1892-1959) was a celebrated Yale baseball, track, and football star who earned his nickname kicking record-breaking field goals. Tall, handsome, and muscular, Lefty himself got kicked out of Yale his senior year after running off to Europe with a Broadway showgirl. At a party in 1914 he met the beautiful, vivacious, 25-year-old Nora Langhorne Phipps (1889-1955), the youngest and most promiscuous of the five infamous Langhorne sisters of Virginia. Despite being married and the mother of two small children, Nora suddenly disappeared with Lefty. Tracked down by her wealthy father, Nora and her family were shipped off to England to live with her well-married sister, Lady Nancy Astor.

Meanwhile, Lefty muddled through two marriages of his own while relying on his rugged good looks to star in nearly forty silent movie Westerns. Eventually, however, his love affair with alcohol cost him his career. In 1930 the two star-crossed lovers met for the first time in fifteen years, prompting Nora to desert her children and husband for a second time. This time she filed for a divorce so that she could marry Lefty.

Attempting to live off her modest family trust fund, in 1934 Nora and Lefty moved to Tryon, far more affordable than Los Angeles or New York, where years earlier she had first met Scott and Zelda at a Manhattan cocktail party. Both Nora and Lefty had professional singing voices and were always the luminaries of any party, especially those they hosted on their horse farm southeast of Tryon named "Little Orchard."

Always searching for the spark of an idea he could fan into his next short story, later in 1935 Scott sold a short story to *McCall's* magazine drawn directly from the lives and marital struggles of Nora and Lefty, entitling it "The Intimate Strangers."

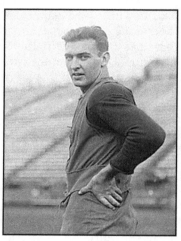

Nora and Maurice 'Lefty' Flynn.

By 1935 Nora had become a Christian Scientist. After convincing Lefty to give up drinking, she set her sights on Scott, but without any success that year. Nora and Lefty later divorced and both moved from Tryon.

Missildine's Drug Store

At 15 South Trade Street, a short walk from the Oak Hall Hotel, stands a building which was once home to Missildine's, a drug store and pharmacy which served soft drinks and ice cream specialties. In 1937 it inspired Scott Fitzgerald to compose a poem dedicated to its banana splits.

The original building on the corner of Trade and Oak Streets was constructed in 1896 for pharmacist E.E. Missildine, who served as Tryon's mayor for several years. After it burned in 1913, Missildine commissioned local architect William E. Strong to design the present three-story structure. When Scott Fitzgerald was staying in Tryon, Missildine's also served as a popular community center, where people came to shop, mingle, chat, and share newspapers from various cities around the country.

Misseldine's (left) on Trade Street. (Photo courtesy the Tryon Bulletin.)

From January through July of 1937 Scott was a regular at Missildine's, where he treated his visiting sixteen-year-old daughter Scottie to banana splits. While it has been assumed that Scott wrote the poem for his daughter, a Spartanburg newspaper reported on August 28, 1977, that he had composed it on a paper napkin while in the drug store with his friend Clara Edwards. According to the article, Clara and Scott often sat together in the drug store during her breaks. On one such occasion, Scott penned a poem on a napkin, which he gave to her.

"I just didn't pay much attention to it," she later confessed in an interview. "In fact, I gave it to a lady who worked in the drug store. It didn't mean a thing to me."

The napkin's current location is unclear, although the 1977 article stated that it was then in Tryon's Lanier Library. Someone, however, did copy the poem for Fitzgerald's fans and local historians:

> *"Oh Missildine's, dear Missildine's,*
> *A dive we'll ne'er forget,*
> *The taste of its banana splits*
> *Is on our tonsils yet.*
> *Its chocolate fudge makes livers budge,*
> *It's really too divine,*
> *And as we reel, we'll give one squeal*
> *For dear old Misseldine's."*

The Pine Crest Inn

Asheville was not the only destination in North Carolina for people in search of relief from tuberculosis. In 1906 the Pine Crest Inn and its three cottages opened outside Tryon as a sanitarium for tuberculosis patients. By 1917, however, owner Carter Brown, a famous Tryon entrepreneur, had converted it into an inn. Among those who are believed to have spent nights at the Pine Crest Inn are both F. Scott Fitzgerald and Ernest Hemingway, though precise dates have not yet been confirmed.

Both Fitzgerald and Hemingway are believed to have stayed in the Swayback Cabin on the grounds. Constructed in Tennessee nearly 250 years ago, the cabin was later dismantled and moved, log by log, to Tryon, where it was reassembled and furnished.

The 1935 Fitzgerald Portrait

In 1935, during his first two weeks in Tryon, Nora introduced Scott to several people, including the artist David Silvette (1909-1992). Born in Richmond, Silvette and his wife vacationed in Tryon, which had then gained a reputation as an artists' colony. Silvette painted a few portraits while staying in Tryon, including one of Fitzgerald in 1935. Fitzgerald reportedly gave Silvette a down-payment of fifty dollars. When he saw the completed painting, Scott pronounced it "swell." However, he did not have the final payment of $200, so Silvette kept the portrait.

(National Portrait Gallery, Washington, DC)

In 1951, Arthur Mizener, a Cornell College professor and author of the first biography of Fitzgerald, tracked down Silvette and purchased the oil painting from him. It now hangs in the National Portrait Gallery in Washington. Dr. Mizener, who like Fitzgerald attended Princeton, is credited with revitalizing interest in F. Scott Fitzgerald with his notable 1951 biography *The Far Side of Paradise*.

Lake Lure:

F. Scott Fitzgerald's Weekend Retreat

36. The Lake Lure Inn

Robert McGoodwin, architect   1927
2771 Memorial Highway   Lake Lure

Conceived and constructed as one of the attractions around the man-made lake, the 1927 Lake Lure Inn is located just two miles from Chimney Rock State Park. The picturesque inn overlooking the lake and a beautiful beach continues to draw people to the foothills of the Blue Ridge Mountains, just as it did in 1935 when F. Scott Fitzgerald alighted from his Asheville taxi in search of solitude, privacy, and inspiration.

Directions from Asheville: Take either I-40 East or I-240 East to Highway 74-A East toward Bat Cave, Chimney Rock, and Lake Lure. Highway 74-A East is a slow, winding but scenic route leading up over the Eastern Continental Divide (elevation 2694') and down the fourteen-mile Hickory Nut Gorge, as it runs alongside the Rocky Broad River toward Lake Lure. The highway literally began as an Indian trail, which then became the Hickory Nut Turnpike and later a stagecoach route connecting Asheville and Charlotte, also known as Drover's Road. Highway 74-A passes through the quaint villages of Bat Cave and Chimney Rock before leading directly to the Lake Lure Inn on the right.

Distance: 28 miles (approximately 45-60 minutes).

Directions from Hendersonville: Take Highway 64 East from downtown Hendersonville or from I-26 toward Bat Cave for fifteen miles. While neither as slow nor as winding as Highway 74-A, this scenic two-lane highway rises up and over a low mountain ridge dotted with apple orchards and roadside stands. At Bat Cave, turn south onto Highway 74-A and drive six miles through Chimney Rock and into the town of Lake Lure. The Lake Lure Inn will be on the right across from the Lake Lure beach.

Distance: 21 miles (approximately 35-45 minutes).

Lake Lure and Chimney Rock

When in 1900 St. Louis physician Dr. Lucius Morse (1871-1946) was diagnosed with tuberculosis, the young man boarded a train for Western North Carolina in search of relief. While staying in a Hendersonville sanitarium, Morse began exploring the mountains east of town by horseback. In the fourteen-mile gorge carved out of the Blue Ridge Mountains by the Rocky Broad River, he came upon the 315-foot monolith called Chimney Rock.

Intrigued, Morse paid owner Jerome "Rome" Freeman twenty-five cents to take him by mule up Chimney Rock Mountain. Freeman, who in 1880 had paid just twenty-five dollars for four hundred acres of surrounding land, had already begun to turn the monolith into a tourist attraction. In 1891 he constructed the first set of stairs leading to the top of Chimney Rock, but when in 1902 Morse offered him $5000 for 64 acres around Chimney Rock, he accepted.

Chimney Rock looking toward Lake Lure.   *(Photo: Lake Lure Inn.)*

With the financial backing of his older twin brothers, Hiram and Asahel, Morse continued buying up property around Chimney Rock and the Rocky Broad River, eventually accumulating nearly one thousand acres of land. His dream was to build not just a tourist attraction but also a residential development, a vacation resort, and a town around a man-made mountain lake he planned to create by constructing a concrete dam across the river. He and his brothers first built a bridge over the Rocky Broad River and a better set of stairs leading to the top, then created hiking trails looping around the mountain. By 1919 the site had grown so popular that the Morse brothers built the Cliff Dwellers, an inn and restaurant on a natural ledge atop Chimney Rock Mountain.

To raise the capital necessary to construct a hydroelectric dam, in 1923 the three brothers formed Chimney Rock Mountains, Inc., selling shares to Asheville investors. The corporation then purchased an additional 8,000 acres around the planned lake, for which Mrs. Morse suggested the name Lake Lure. The stockholders also formed the Carolina Mountain Power Company and in 1925 began construction of a dam at Tumbling Shoals on the Rocky Broad River. The plan was to create a picturesque 720-acre lake around which they would sell residential and commercial building lots, while at the same time generating power from the hydroelectric dam.

Fed by the Rocky Broad River, Buffalo Creek, Cane Creek, and several natural springs, the lake had filled by 1927. At the western end, alongside the Asheville-Charlotte Highway, that same year the corporation opened a public beach, the three-story Lake Lure Inn, and an adjacent business building, each reflecting an architectural style reminiscent of northern Italy. Adding to the attraction, which already was drawing more than 30,000 tourists a year, was a new golf course designed by Donald Ross. As a result, the town of Lake Lure was officially incorporated in 1927.

Two years later, however, the stock market crash derailed the Morse brothers' and their investors' ambitious plans for additional hotels, residential neighborhoods, and resort businesses around Lake Lure. Two mortgage companies foreclosed on the corporation, which was forced to liquidate its holdings. The Carolina Mountain Power Company eventually purchased the entire lake and operated the dam until 1965, when ownership of both the dam and the lake was transferred to the town of Lake Lure.

Despite the setback, the Morse family was able to retain ownership of Chimney Rock Park and operated it for several more decades. Dr. Lucius Morse passed away in 1946 at the age of seventy-five, finally succumbing to the tuberculosis which had brought him to the area. He was buried in the cemetery of the Chimney Rock Baptist Church, where his tombstone faces his beloved Chimney Rock.

The Morse descendants continued to operate Chimney Rock Park as a tourist attraction during and after the Great Depression. In 1934 they

135.

commissioned Art Deco architect Douglas Ellington, who had previously designed four significant Art Deco buildings in Asheville, to design a new entrance on Highway 74-A in Chimney Rock Village. Originally the building was utilized as both administrative offices and for ticket sales, but after numerous traffic jams a new ticket office was constructed further up the road leading to Chimney Rock. In 2007, the Morse family sold the 996-acre park to the state of North Carolina for $24 million.

The combination of a temperate climate, panoramic views from the top of Chimney Rock, the tranquil lake nestled amid towering granite cliffs, and a growing number of shops, restaurants, and activities continues to attract weekend tourists, seasonal residents, and full-time homeowners to the three villages of Bat Cave, Chimney Rock, and Lake Lure.

It has also drawn a number of movie crews, beginning in 1958 with the filming of "Thunder Road," followed by "A Breed Apart" (1984), "Firestarter" (1984), "Dirty Dancing" (1987), "My Fellow Americans" (1996), "The Last of the Mohicans" (1992), and "Careful What You Wish For" (2015). Cast and crew members often stayed at the historic 1927 Lake Lure Inn.

A promotional photo of the 1927 Lake Lure Inn.   *(Photo courtesy of the Lake Lure Inn.)*

136.

F. Scott Fitzgerald at the Lake Lure Inn

F. Scott Fitzgerald's hopeful summer of 1935 turned sour when he let himself become deeply involved with Beatrice Dance, a young, attractive but married mother from Memphis who was vacationing with her sister at the Grove Park Inn. Their affair began that June and soon was discovered by Beatrice's sister, who called her brother-in-law, imploring him to come to Asheville. Learning this, Scott was shaken, fearing a physical altercation with her angry husband.

On July 14 Beatrice declared her love for Scott, offering to leave her husband and daughter, willing to support Scott while he worked to rebuild his literary career. Her husband, Dupree "Hop" Dance, arrived in Asheville the following day, prompting Scott to begin making plans to leave the city. Having heard of the Lake Lure Inn, he arranged to take a taxi there on Friday, July 19. He remained at the inn until Monday, when he returned to Asheville and immediately boarded a train for New York.

Front entrance.　　*(Photo by James Willamor, Wikimedia Creative Commons.)*

The white plastered, three-story Lake Lure Inn, with an open veranda and arched, floor-to-ceiling first floor windows, still looks today as if it had been designed by an Italian architect. A wide set of steps leads up from the circular drive to a massive front door and opens to a long perpendicular lobby with an ornate mahogany bar and formal dining room overlooking Lake Lure. An impressive open staircase extends up through the center of the building to guest rooms on the second and third floors. Today the lobby is decorated with American and European antiques, as well as artifacts and photographs relating to the Inn's history.

Earlier that summer, soon after arriving at the Grove Park Inn, Scott had completed a short story entitled "Zone of Accident," which appeared in the *Saturday Evening Post* on July 13 and for which he received $3,000. After meeting fortune-teller Laura Guthrie at the Grove Park Inn, in June he began writing "Fate In Her Hands." He may well have brought the manuscript with him to the Lake Lure Inn when he arrived late in the afternoon of Friday, July 19.

If his routine at the Grove Park Inn was any indication, Scott most likely requested an upper floor overlooking the front entrance, made his way to the ornate mahogany bar in the lobby, and ate dinner either in the hotel's dining room or ordered room service. If he was putting the finishing touches on "Fate In Her Hands" or making notes for his next story "Image On the Heart," Scott would have risen early on Saturday and Sunday, ordered a pot of black coffee, and began writing in his room. By mid-afternoon, especially given the self-inflicted emotional stress he was suffering, he would have switched to either beer, straight gin, or both. A few weeks later he confessed to a friend:

"I have just emerged not totally unscathed, I'm afraid, from a short violent love affair . . . I had done much better to let it alone because this was scarcely a time in my life for one more emotion. Still it's done now – and maybe someday I'll get a chapter out of it. I am still swollen up like a barrel, but have reduced my beer consumption to nine bottles today."

Scott often grew restless after a day of writing in his room, so it was not surprising that he walked down to the Lake Lure beach on Saturday afternoon. As his friend, confidant, and occasional typist Laura Guthrie noted in her journal for that day, "Said he had tried to get a little sun during the day, but was not at all equal to going into the water. Another day he told me that he had tried to get sunburned to disguise the growing air of dissipation that he had." She added:

"Scott called me at 1:30am. For he was nearly crazy alone at Lake Lure and wanted me to come down for a day and do some work with him. But as I did not wake, he made other plans, which were to come to Asheville and to go to New York the next day. For my sake, too, I was glad to have him going to such a distance that he could not call me at midnight or ask me to do things for him. He is such a creature of moods, even if they come in the middle of the night. And he is getting to the place when drink has made it impossible for him to sleep and so he wants someone with him, just to listen and not even talk."

On Saturday, Scott sent Laura a postcard from the inn, declaring:

"Gradually putting things together. Should have stayed at the 'Rocky Broad Inn' across the street, but there might have been no broads there at the moment, and besides I've been feeling plenty rocky myself at this one."

His July 1935 weekend at Lake Lure and Chimney Rock provided Scott with the backdrop for a short story he completed upon his return to Baltimore that November. Called "I'd Die For You," it opens:

"Within a cup of the Carolina mountains lay the lake, a pink glow of summer evening on its surface. In the lake was a peninsula and on this an Italian hotel of stucco turned to many colors with the progress of the sun."

Subtitled "The Legend of Lake Lure," the story revolves around a Hollywood film crew whose starlet meets a mysterious gentleman at the hotel.

"I'm sort of a survival from the boom days -- I've lived too long."
"Sort of a luxury article," suggested Roger mildly.
"That's it. Not much in demand any more."

The dark story reflects Fitzgerald's ruminations on suicide, which prompted the *Saturday Evening Post* and other magazines to reject it, for their readers were more accustomed to Fitzgerald's lighter stories of young love. Details in the story indicate that Scott had toured the beach, the town, and Chimney Rock, "which is a great monolith breaking off from the mountains like the spout of a teapot."

In April of 1936, soon after he had transferred her to Highland Hospital, Scott drove Zelda down to Chimney Rock in his 1927 Packard. As a child, Zelda and her family had vacationed in Chimney Rock, staying in a boarding house which she and Scott tried unsuccessfully to find that day. Even so, he remarked, "Sometimes one would never know she is ill."

During the summer of 1935, possibly at the Lake Lure Inn, Scott began formulating two autobiographical short stories, "Image On the Heart" and "Too Cute For Words." These were the final stories for which the *Saturday Evening Post* would again pay him $3,000 – a remarkable sum during the Great Depression. During the next and final three years of his life, he wrote almost exclusively for *Esquire* magazine. *Esquire*, however, only paid $250 per article or story, but it enabled Scott to survive while working on his final novel, *The Last Tycoon*, which remained uncompleted when Scott died in Hollywood of a heart attack on December 21, 1940.

He was just forty-four years old.

Thomas Wolfe and Scott Fitzgerald:
An Uneasy Friendship

"I may be wrong, but all I can get out of it is that you think I'd be a good writer if I were an altogether different writer from the writer that I am."
— Tom Wolfe to Scott Fitzgerald, 1937

Three of the most important literary figures of the first half of the twentieth century – F. Scott Fitzgerald, Ernest Hemingway, and Thomas Wolfe – shared a common bond through their influential editor Maxwell Perkins.

After graduating from Harvard in 1907, Maxwell Perkins (1884-1947) went to work at Charles Scribner's Sons in 1910. At that time the conservative New York publishing house only worked with established authors, but in 1920 Perkins persuaded Charles Scribner to take a chance on a fresh novel by the unknown writer Francis Scott Fitzgerald, eventually entitled *This Side of Paradise*.

A grateful Fitzgerald later recommended Ernest Hemingway to his editor, who convinced his colleagues at Scribner's that Hemingway's *The Sun Also Rises*, despite its profanity and sparse style of writing, could become a best-seller for the firm, which it did in 1926.

A few years later Perkins would also be struggling to convince a young and headstrong Tom Wolfe that his massive manuscript for *Look Homeward, Angel* would benefit from some extensive cutting, revision, and reorganization.

The father of five daughters, Maxwell Perkins, though not much

Maxwell Perkins. (Photo courtesy of Princeton University Library and Charles Scribner's Sons.)

older than his famous trio of writers, often treated them like sons. He also encouraged them to meet with each other whenever possible and, hopefully, to become friendly advisers. Unfortunately, whether because of diverse personalities, contrasting styles, or simple literary jealousy, the three writers never grew close.

In June of 1930, knowing both writers were staying in Paris, Maxwell Perkins encouraged Wolfe and Fitzgerald to meet for the first time. Tom was about to turn thirty and Scribner's had just published *Look Homeward, Angel*. Though only four years older, Scott had already risen to fame on his best-selling *This Side of Paradise*, edited by Perkins and published by Scribner's when he was just twenty-four years old. Perkins may well have hoped that Scott's recognition of the necessity to remove extemporaneous material from his fiction would rub off on Tom. *Look Homeward, Angel* had arrived at Perkin's office as an enormous 330,000-word manuscript. Only after months of heated arguments had Tom reluctantly consented to the removal of approximately 66,000 words – 20,000 more words than the entire manuscript of *The Great Gatsby*.

The Ritz Bar in Paris had become a literary hangout for American and international authors and their admirers, most famously Scott Fitzgerald and Ernest Hemingway. Scott, burdened by Zelda's recent hospitalization in Switzerland for a nervous breakdown and his own inability to complete a sequel to *The Great Gatsby*, already sensed that Wolfe and Hemingway might well replace him as Scribner's rising stars. When Tom arrived that night at the Ritz Bar, Scott was already encircled by a group of young admirers. The two writers met, but Tom elected not to stay late.

"I finally departed from his company at ten that night in the Ritz Bar," he explained to Perkins, "where he was entirely surrounded by Princeton boys, all nineteen years old, all drunk, and all half-raw."

If Perkins had hoped Tom's meeting with Scott would inspire the younger writer to be more open to reducing the length of his manuscripts, he was disappointed. After reading *Look Homeward, Angel*, Scott had written Perkins, "Have spent twenty consecutive hours with your first book. Am enormously moved and grateful. He strikes me as a man who should be let alone as to length, [even] if he has to be published in five volumes. I liked him enormously."

As it turns out, however, the feeling was not mutual.

A few weeks after meeting for the first time in Paris, Tom was living and writing in a quiet Swiss hotel overlooking Lake Geneva, where he was working on *Of Time and the River*. Upon spotting Scott and another young man, Tom waved them over to his table. The threesome first did a small amount of gambling at a nearby casino, then followed Scott to a nightclub.

141.

Tom reported back to Perkins, "This sounds much gayer than it is: there is very little to do here. Later Scott and his friend drove back to Vevey, a village a mile or so from here on the lake; they are staying there. They asked me to come over and dine with them, but I am not going. I do not think I am very good company to people at present. When I am with someone like Scott, I feel that I am morose and sullen – and violent in my speech and movement part of the time – later I feel that I have repelled them."

Perkins wrote back a few weeks later, "I'm glad you saw Scott, but he's in trouble: Zelda is still very seriously ill in a nervous breakdown. I don't know how it will end. Scott is blamable, I know, for what has come to Zelda, in a sense. But he's a brave man to face trouble as he does, always facing it squarely – no self-deceptions."

Ernest Hemingway had come to know both Scott and Zelda from their early days in Paris at the Ritz Bar. While he and Scott always remained cordial, Zelda and Ernest took an instant dislike to each other. In 1932 Hemingway wrote to Perkins: "Poor old Scott. He should have swapped Zelda when she was at her craziest, but still salable five or six years ago, before she was diagnosed as nutty. He is the great tragedy in our bloody generation . . . ."

In late 1932 or early 1933 Ernest Hemingway and Tom Wolfe also met one another, which naturally pleased Perkins, who again hoped one of his writers could convince Tom of the value of careful editing. Hemingway wrote back, "He was awfully nice. He is like a great child and you must remember that. Geniuses of that sort I guess are always children. Children, as you may have observed, Mr. Perkins, are a hell of a responsibility. I liked him very, very much. He has a great talent and a very delicate fine spirit. You've got to be a big part of his intelligence, so for Christ sake don't lose his confidence."

Scott also reported back to Perkins after his evening with Tom in Switzerland: "You have a great find in him – what he'll do is incalculable. He has a deeper culture than Ernest and more vitality; if he is slightly less of a poet, that goes with the immense surface he wants to cover. Also he lacks Ernest's quality of a stick hardened in the fire – he is more susceptible to the world. John Bishop [an American poet] told me he needed advice about cutting, etc., but after reading his book I thought that was nonsense."

In addition to simply not warming to Fitzgerald's personality, Tom grew to distrust Scott, accurately sensing he was reporting his activities back to Perkins and other friends in New York City.

"You are my friend," Tom wrote to Perkins in December of 1930, "and one of the two or three people that I would not let anyone in the world say a word against, so until I get back at least don't listen to opinions and judgments from people who don't know a God damned thing about me, whether Scott Fitzgerald or anyone else."

Privately, Tom held Perkins partially responsible for his awkward encounters with Scott. In his personal notebook he wrote the following regarding their two meetings in Europe in 1930:

"There was once a young man who came to have a feeling of great trust and devotion for an older man [Perkins]. He thought that this older man had created liberty and hope for him. He thought this older man was brave and loyal. Then he found that this older man had sent him to a drunken and malicious fellow, who tried to injure and hurt his work in every way possible. He found moreover that this older man had sent him to this drunk in order to get the drunk's 'opinion' of him."

The third meeting between Wolfe and Fitzgerald was also arranged by Maxwell Perkins. For the first six months of 1934 Perkins and Tom struggled, fought, and wrestled with the ungainly manuscript which slowly took shape as *Of Time and the River.* As Tom had written in December of 1933 when he delivered the manuscript, "Buried in that great pile of manuscript is some of the best writing I have ever done. Let's see to it that it does not go to waste."

That June of 1934 Perkins arranged a luncheon for the three of them. Scott, who was spending most of his time in Baltimore where Zelda was a patient at Sheppard-Pratt Hospital, often came up to New York to visit friends. Nine years after *The Great Gatsby*, Fitzgerald's long-awaited *Tender Is the Night* had just been released, but the reviews had not been favorable. Tom, however, had written Scott in 1934, praising the novel as "the best work you've done so far, and I know you'll understand what I mean and won't mind if I get a kind of selfish hope and joy out of your own success."

"Thanks a hell of a lot for your letter," Scott replied, "which came at a rather sunken moment and was the more welcome."

At their June luncheon, Perkins carefully guided the conversation to the subject of Wolfe's current manuscript. "You tell Tom to cut something and a great hand comes over and slowly crosses out a word," he joked to Scott. "But you tell him to improve it, to add to it, and the words just flow." Following Perkins' lead, Scott advised Tom, "You never cut anything out of a book that you regret later." Tom remained unconvinced.

Privately, Scott proved critical of Tom's abundant use of long descriptive passages. "He who has such infinite power of suggestion and delicacy," he wrote in 1935, "has absolutely no right to glut people on whole meals of caviar. Athletes have got to learn their games; they shouldn't just be content to tense their muscles and, if they do, they suddenly find when called upon to bring off a necessary effect they are simply liable to hurl the shot into the crowd and not break any records at all."

To yet another young writer, Scott passed on this piece of advice, at Tom's expense: "Form is literary discipline. It takes planning and clear thinking, a sense of restraint, and a wise selection of material. This is something Wolfe's work lacks . . . ."

Much to Tom's dismay, Perkins soon sent the manuscript for *Of Time and the River* to the printer without giving Tom the additional six months he had requested to continue revising it. On July 4, 1935, Tom returned to New York after a four-month sojourn in Europe, arriving this time as an acclaimed author riding the wave of success created by his second novel. That evening Perkins, who had greeted Tom at the pier, took him out to a celebratory dinner. Coincidentally, Scott was on a trip back from North Carolina and happened to be at the same restaurant. Scott briefly stopped by their table "with a rather disreputable-looking blonde." Seeing his editor of fifteen years out to dinner on the Fourth of July with Scribner's next rising star, celebrating their successful second novel together and making plans for a third, could not have elicited much genuine praise from the always-envious Scott, who quickly scurried away.

Their fifth and final meeting took place in North Carolina. On May 2, 1937, after an absence of eight years since the publication of *Look Homeward, Angel*, Tom stepped off the bus in Asheville and hailed a cab to his mother's boarding house on Spruce Street. Undoubtedly at Maxwell Perkins' urging, Tom soon inquired about getting someone to drive him to Tryon to pay a visit to Scott, who had fled there after checking out of his more expensive rooms at the Grove Park Inn.

The forty-year-old author, who had once lived with Zelda in a luxurious suite at the Plaza Hotel in New York City, had since been reduced to a cramped, dollar-a-day room in a small-town hotel, attempting to dry out enough to be hired as a screenwriter for M-G-M in Hollywood.

Knowing that Tom was going to be in Asheville for two weeks, Fred Wolfe took time off work and offered to drive his brother around town. "Well, that's mighty nice of you," Tom replied, "and I'll just take you up on it. There are two friends down here I'd like to see. One of them is a fellow who has had a lot of hard luck with his life; he's the one I wrote you about last fall, Fred. He was staying at Grove Park Inn then, but now he's down at Oak Hall in Tryon; he's Scott Fitzgerald."

The prior year Tom had written Fred: "There is a poor, desperate, unhappy man staying at the Grove Park Inn. He is a man of great talent but is throwing it away on drink and worry over his misfortune . . . . His name, I forgot to say, is Scott Fitzgerald."

Fred agreed, and on Wednesday, May 5, the three Wolfe siblings and mother Julia climbed into Fred's car for the winding forty-five-mile trip down Highway 25 to Tryon. Mabel's recollections of the day were later recorded in the book *Thomas Wolfe and His Family*. The four stopped for lunch in Hendersonville, arriving at the Oak Hall Hotel at 1:30pm, where Scott was waiting for them on the wide, covered veranda perched high above Trade Street.

Scott, who declared he had not had a drink since December, provided Fred and Tom with two glasses and a bottle of gin, but declined any himself. "I'm off it like a dirty shirt," he declared. "I can't take the stuff." As Mabel recalled,

"He was very pleasant and courteous and I was quite favorably impressed with him. He and Tom had been talking about books and the subject of Margaret Mitchell's monumental Gone With the Wind came up; it had been out almost a year then and already had sold into astounding figures.

Fred joined in, 'Have you read it yet, Scott?'

'Yes, Fred, I have. I've read every word of it. I read it in about two hours' time, and I don't think I found two good paragraphs in the whole book. What do you think about it, Tom?'

'I intend to read it,' came the reply, 'but I haven't read it yet. It's too damned long.'

And then Fred, good old Fred, spoke out. 'Well, I don't know how good it is,' he declared, looking evenly at Fitzgerald. 'But there's one thing sure. I wish you and Tom could write a book that would make the money that Margaret Mitchell's making on that one.'"

In 1955, while writing *The French Broad*, author Wilma Dykeman included another recollection from this meeting between Fitzgerald and Wolfe. It, too, may have come Mabel Wolfe Wheaton, who died in 1958. Dykeman inadvertently assumed the meeting took place at the Grove Park Inn, since Scott had spent most of the last two years there:

"When Tom Wolfe revisited Asheville in 1937, F. Scott Fitzgerald was in town at the same time, stopping by the Grove Park Inn, the handsome resort hotel built by Bromo-quinine king, E.W. Grove. They got together, of course, and talked. At last Fitzgerald said, 'This is a sterile town, Tom. Why do you come here for characters?'

And Wolfe replied, 'What are you talking about, Scott? I've just come from Burnsville over in Yancey County. I've been talking with my mother's uncle, John Westall, over there. He's ninety-five, he was at [the Civil War battle of] Chickamauga and he told me about it. My God, it was wonderful. I'm going to write it all down verbatim. There's your character, Scott, back in Yancey County. What did you expect to find up here at the Grove Park Inn? They're the same people you see at expensive hotels everywhere. But you go out in these mountains here . . . . Sterile, Scott? Don't you believe it!'"

When the time came for the Wolfe family to start back home, Mabel recalled a final conversation between Scott and Tom:

"'Tom,' Scott asked my brother just as we were getting ready to leave, 'how old are you now?'
'Why, Scott,' Tom said, 'I'll soon be thirty-seven.'
'My God, Tom, I'm forty. Look, bud,' he said, suddenly very serious, 'we're at a dangerous age. You know in this country we burn ourselves out at the work we are doing, and this is particularly true of writers.'"

Scott remained at the Oak Hall Hotel for the remainder of the month, but the two men made no other attempt to get together again. By the time Tom returned to Asheville in July, Scott had accepted a job as a screenwriter for M-G-M in California. Despite the distance between them, Scott remained convinced he could help Tom become a better writer, advising him to tone down the pitch of some of his more descriptive, more emotional passages. On July 17, from his apartment in Los Angeles, Scott wrote in part to Tom:

"I think I could make out a good case for your necessity to cultivate an alter ego, a more conscious artist in you. Hasn't it occurred to you that such qualities as pleasantness or grief, exuberance or cynicism can become a plague on others? That often people who live at a high pitch often don't get their way emotionally at the important moment because it doesn't stand out in relief?

Now the more that the stronger man's inner tendencies are defined, the more he can be sure they will show, the more necessity to rarify them, to use them sparingly. To a talent like more of narrow scope, there is not that problem. I must put everything in to have enough and even then I often haven't got enough.

That in brief is my case against you, if it can be called that, when I admire you so much and think your talent is unmatchable in this or any other country."

Tom must have stewed over Scott's letter before answering him at great length on July 26. Part of his reply read:

"The unexpected loquaciousness of your letter street me all of a heap. I was surprised to hear from you, but I don't know that I can truthfully say I was delighted. Your bouquet arrived smelling sweetly of roses, but cunningly concealing several large-sized brick-bats.

146.

I'm not sore at you or sore about anything you said in your letter. And if there is any truth in what you say – any truth for me – you can depend upon it I shall probably get it out. It just seems to me that there is not much in what you say. You speak of your "case" against me, and frankly I don't believe you have much case. I have read your letter several times and I've got to admit it doesn't seems to mean much.

I may be wrong, but all I can get out of it is that you think I'd be a good writer if I were an altogether different writer from the writer that I am.

This either-or kind of criticism seems to me to be so meaningless. It looks so knowing and imposing but there is nothing in it, for your argument is based simply upon one way, upon one method instead of another. And have you ever noticed how often it turns out that what a man is really doing is simply rationalizing his own way of doing something, the way he has to do it, the way given him by his talent and his nature into the only inevitable and right way of doing everything?

I am going into the woods for another two or three years. I am going to try to do the best, the most important piece of work I have ever done. I am going to have to do it alone. I am going to lose what little bit of reputation I have gained, to have to hear and know and endure in silence again all of the doubt, the disparagement, the ridicule, the post-mortems that they are so eager to read over you even before you are dead. I know what it means and so do you.

Good bye, Scott, and good luck."

A little more than a year after their final meeting, a week after Scott had learned of Tom's death on September 15, 1938, Scott wrote to Maxwell Perkins:

"I read in the papers that he was starting East sick. This worried me and it seemed a very forlorn and desolate and grievous experience, yet something which his great vitality would somehow transcend and dominate – and then the end at Baltimore and that great pulsing, vital frame quiet at last.

There is a great hush after him . . . ."

Tom and Scott: A Writer's Craft

Two successful novelists could not have had more different approaches to writing than Thomas Wolfe and F. Scott Fitzgerald.

Soon after a newspaper article appeared with a photograph of the six-foot-six-inch Wolfe writing longhand on top of a refrigerator in one of the many apartments he rented, reporters liked to assume this is how Tom always wrote. While that one small refrigerator did provide him with a smooth surface on which to write, his sister Mabel Wolfe Wheaton observed, "How much writing he did on top of that refrigerator I really don't know; I suspect it was considerably less than the stories about it indicate."

Ed Aswell, his editor at Harper's, had watched Tom work and shared this observation:

"There was a big table in the living room of this suite, and on the table was a huge stack of yellow second sheets which he used for his manuscript writing. Beside it was an enormous pile of pencils, which his secretary sharpened every morning. He sat there writing away in his great gargantuan scrawl with about six to eight lines on a page, and as he would write and finish a page, he would grab it with his left hand and shove it to the floor, take a new page from the stack and go on.

The floor was littered with sheets containing his writing. None of the sheets was numbered; it was his secretary's job to pick the sheets up and by the internal evidence put them in order, and then type them out."

Wolfe once told his literary agent, "I can always find plenty of women to sleep with, but the kind of woman that is really hard for me to find is a typist who can read my writing."

After the 1935 publication of his second novel *Of Time and the River*, Tom accumulated wooden crates of both handwritten and typed pages which would become his third and fourth novels. In May of 1937, after spending two weeks in Asheville, he returned to his apartment in New York to organize "a tremendous manuscript he had accumulated, millions of words, thousands of pages." Unsure whether he would go back to his apartment, Tom shipped ahead to his mother's boarding house on Spruce Street "a huge packing case that contained, as he expressed it, his veritable life – years and years of work and sweating blood."

When he was sober and working, Wolfe's output was staggering. While Ernest Hemingway often stated that he was pleased to write between 500-1,000 words a day, Tom was once seen striding up and down the street in front of his New York apartment chanting, "I wrote 10,000 words today . . . . I wrote 10,000 words today."

Unlike Hemingway and Fitzgerald, who both wrote best in the morning, Tom tended to sleep until late morning, then would write throughout the afternoon and into the evening, often followed by some late-night drinking with friends.

During the time Fitzgerald lived at the Grove Park Inn, he worked erratically, often finding feeble excuses for not writing. In his defense, he was besieged with financial worries, from making payments for Scottie's private schooling to the high cost of the private sanitariums Zelda had been a patient in since 1930. Nevertheless, Scott's volume of letters demonstrates that he invested far more time and creative energy writing personal letters than lucrative short stories.

Thomas Wolfe Collection, Pack Memorial Library.

When he was focused on a story, Scott typically started each day with a pot of black coffee brought to his room at the Grove Park Inn. By late morning he had switched to beer, hiding the empty bottles in the closet by the door. His only lunch would be a thin soup. When the beer no longer heightened the emotions he felt he needed to compose a good story, Scott turned to straight gin. A regular visitor reported:

"I found him in his pajamas and an old dressing gown he often wore while working. There were papers on the table and couch; he reached for a pencil behind his ear while mulling over the rough draft of a story. There were circles under his eyes, his face was pallid, his beer belly protruded. Books, clothes, and papers were scattered about, ash trays piled with butts and bits of rubbish; and there were bottles, all empty but one, which was half-full of gin, and cups, bowls, and an ornate silver coffeepot on a room-service tray precariously set near a closet door. The door was ajar; there was a large carton of empty bottles on the floor."

"The Jazz Age is over," he wrote to Maxwell Perkins. "I wish I had these great masses of manuscripts stored away like Wolfe, but this goose is beginning to be pretty thoroughly plucked."

An Asheville woman hired to type his manuscripts in the summer of 1936 recalled her days with Scott at the Grove Park Inn:

"I am sure, though, that he felt his writing ability had left, or was leaving him for good. He brooded on this, and tried so desperately hard to write, and the result was largely trash, as he well knew. He wrote and re-wrote and re-re-wrote some stories, none of which was much good. There were periods when he was trying to write and considerable lengths of time when he made no attempt. When he did try, it was more or less in a frenzy. There was much more time, I should say, when he was making no effort than when he was. He does work, but only very little – maybe three, four hours a week.

Sometimes he was gay and talkative and utterly charming. At others he was tragically depressed. Meals were sent up to his rooms and Dorothy [his nurse] and I did our level best to get him to eat, but I never saw him take more than a few bites. Apparently, he lived on gin and beer – that is what he drank all the time I was there. I have no idea how much gin he averaged a day, but it was plenty."

Near what turned out to be the final months of his life, Scott wrote in a letter to Zelda in 1940: "It's odd that my old talent for the short story vanished. It was partly that times changed, editors changed, but part of it was tied up somehow with you and me – the happy ending. Essentially I got my public with stories of young love."

When Tom Wolfe died in 1938 at the age of thirty-seven, he left behind enough manuscripts for his editor to shape into two novels, *The Web and The Rock* (1939) and *You Can't Go Home Again* (1940), plus a collection of short stories, *The Hills Beyond* (1941).

Two years later, Scott Fitzgerald died of a heart attack at the age of forty-four. At the time he was well into the first draft of a novel set in Hollywood. The partial manuscript was turned over to writer and literary critic Edmund Wilson, a close friend of Scott's, who prepared the unfinished *The Last Tycoon* for publication in 1941.

"You are an artist," Tom had written to Scott Fitzgerald in 1937, "and an artist has the only true critical intelligence. You have had to work and sweat blood yourself, and you know what it is like to try to write a living word or create a living thing."

Thomas Clayton Wolfe:
A Timeline

1885 - January 14 - William Oliver Wolfe (1851-1922) and Julia Westall (1860-1945) are married in Asheville and move into the home he had built at 92 Woodfin Street in Asheville.

1900 - October 3 - Thomas Clayton Wolfe, their seventh surviving child, is born at their home.

1906 - August 30 - Julia Wolfe purchases the Old Kentucky Home at 48 Spruce Street, two blocks away. She moves into the house with six-year-old Tom.

1906 - September - Tom enters the Orange Street Public School a few blocks away.

1912 - September - Tom enrolls in the private North State Fitting School at 157 Church Street run by John and Margaret Roberts. He called these four years "the happiest and most valuable years of my life."

1916 - September - At age sixteen, Tom enters the University of North Carolina at Chapel Hill. He already stood six-feet-three-inches tall, weighed just 135 pounds, and was still growing.

1918 - October 19 - Ben, age twenty-six and Tom's closest sibling, dies of pneumonia brought on by the Spanish influenza epidemic. His lungs had already been weakened by exposure to tuberculosis, most likely contracted from one of his mother's dubious boarders.

1920 - June 16 - Tom graduates from the University of North Carolina, which he called "the magical campus." That fall Tom enrolls in Harvard University's Graduate School of Arts. He displays the first symptoms of latent tuberculosis in his right lung.

1922 - June 20 - William Oliver Wolfe, age seventy-one, dies of prostate cancer in their boarding house.

1924 - February - After earning his master's degree from Harvard, Tom begins teaching at New York University. He continues teaching for six years, during which time he makes the first of his seven trips to Europe.

1925 - August 25 - On his way back from Europe, Tom meets Aline Bernstein, a married set designer, with whom he begins a tumultuous seven-year affair.

1926 - July - With Aline's encouragement and financial support, Tom begins writing *Look Homeward, Angel* while in Europe.

1927 - January - Upon his return to New York, Tom continues to write *Look Homeward, Angel* as he resumes teaching.

1928 - March - Tom finishes what becomes *Look Homeward, Angel*. That October Maxwell Perkins, chief editor at Charles Scribner's Sons, encourages him to revise and shorten it.

1929 - September 7 - Tom visits his family in Asheville for a few days but does not adequately prepare them for their portrayal in the novel. He does not return again for eight years.

1929- October 18 - Scribner's releases *Look Homeward, Angel* to mixed reviews. He soon resigns his teaching position.

1930 - June - While in Paris, Tom meets Scott and Zelda Fitzgerald at the urging of Maxwell Perkins.

1931 - March - Tom takes an apartment in Brooklyn to write full-time.

1933 - January - Tom continues working on the manuscript that will become *Of Time and the River*.

1934 - June - Maxwell Perkins arranges for Tom and Scott to have lunch with him in New York.

1935 - March 8 - Frustrated with Tom's overdue revisions, Perkins releases *Of Time and the River* while he is abroad.

1935 - July 4 - Tom returns to New York as a literary celebrity; he and Perkins runs into Scott at dinner.

1935 - November 14 - Tom's collection of short stories called *From Death to Morning* is published by Scribner's.

1936 - April 21 - Tom's non-fiction *The Story of a Novel* is released and attacked by critics.

1937 - Spring - Tom begins suffering severe headaches. Accompanied by reoccurring colds, exhaustion, and the flu, all danger signs to someone predisposed for tuberculosis, Tom has a new will drawn in April.

1937 - May 1 - On his way back to Asheville, Tom stays overnight at the Nu-Wray Inn in Burnsville, NC, where he witnesses a shooting on Main Street. Later that summer he is called back to testify in the trial.

1937 - May 3-15 - Tom arrives in Asheville by bus for a two-week stay at his mother's Old Kentucky Home, but is beset with visitors. He spends time walking the streets of Asheville with friends and a newspaper reporter before returning to New York. A former classmate, Max Whitson, offers to rent Tom a cabin outside Asheville for $30 a month upon his return in July.

1937 - May 5 - Tom, Fred, Mabel and their mother drive to the Oak Hall Hotel in Tryon to spend the afternoon with Scott Fitzgerald.

1937 - July 2 - Tom returns to Asheville and moves into the furnished cabin situated on fifteen acres of land southeast of town. Despite its rural location, Tom still has daily visitors while he attempts to complete a short story entitled "The Party at Jack's."

1937 - July - Tom exchanges letters with Scott, who had just moved to Los Angeles to write for M-G-M.

1937 - August 16 - Tom is summoned back to Burnsville to testify in the trial of the man involved in the shooting he had witnessed. He checks into the Nu-Wray Inn on the 16th and testifies the following day. Tom then returns to Asheville, gets drunk, and spends the night sobering up in the Asheville jail. No charges are filed against him.

1937 - August 18 - Seeking privacy, Tom leaves the cabin and checks into the downtown Battery Park Hotel.

1937 - September 2 - Tom leaves Asheville and moves back to New York.

1937 - December 31 - Tom officially ends his relationship with Maxwell Perkins and Scribner's, switching to Harper and Brothers, where his new editor is Edward Aswell.

1938 - May 17 - Tom finishes a lengthy manuscript submitted as *George Webber*, which later becomes *The Web and the Rock*, then plans a vacation in the Northwest.

1938 - July 5 - While traveling on a ferry to Seattle, Tom contracts a respiratory infection, activating tuberculosis cells lodged in his right lung since growing up in his mother's boarding house. He remains hospitalized in Washington for several weeks.

1938 - September 10 - Tom's family takes him to Johns Hopkins Hospital in Baltimore, where on September 12th surgeons perform an exploratory operation on his skull. They determine Tom cannot survive for more than a few days.

1938 - September 15 - Tom dies early in the morning a little more than two weeks before his 38th birthday. The cause of death is listed as tuberculous meningitis brought on by acute pulmonary tuberculosis. After his funeral in the First Presbyterian Church, Tom is buried in Asheville's Riverside Cemetery.

1939 - June 22 - *The Web and the Rock*, edited by Edward Aswell, is published by Harper and Brothers.

1940 - September 18 - *You Can't Go Home Again*, also edited by Edward Aswell, is published by Harper and Brothers.

1949 - July 19 - The Old Kentucky Home boarding house is opened to the public as a museum. Renewed interest in Thomas Wolfe has since led to the publication of additional short stories, letters, and personal journals the prolific writer had left in his infamous crates.

Zelda and F. Scott Fitzgerald:
A Timeline

1896 - September 24 - Francis Scott Key Fitzgerald is born in St. Paul, Minnesota.

1900 - July 24 - Zelda Sayre is born in Montgomery, Alabama.

1913 - September - Scott enrolls in Princeton University. Four years later he leaves without graduating.

1917 - October - Scott enlists in the army. While on leave the next spring he finishes the first draft of *This Side of Paradise*.

1918 - July - Scott is stationed at Fort Sheridan, near Montgomery, where he meets Zelda Sayre at a dance.

1919 - February - The war ends with Scott never having left the states, which he regrets. He takes a job with an ad agency in New York, while making regular train trips to Montgomery to see Zelda.

1919 - August - Scott returns to his parents' home in St. Paul where finishes his novel. He sends it to New York, where editor Maxwell Perkins convinces Charles Scribner to publish it as *This Side of Paradise*.

1920 - March - Scribner's releases *This Side of Paradise* which makes the best-seller list. Zelda accepts Scott's marriage proposal.

1920 - April 3 - Scott, then twenty-three, and Zelda, just nineteen, are married in New York City. Scott begins work on several short stories.

1920 - September - His short story collection *Flappers and Philosophers* is released.

1921 - January - Zelda becomes pregnant; that May they go to Europe.

1921 - October 26 - The Fitzgerald's only child, Frances Scott 'Scottie' Fitzgerald, is born in St. Paul.

1922 - March - Scott's second novel, *The Beautiful and the Damned*, edited by Maxwell Perkins and published by Scribner's, receives positive reviews, which leads to strong sales.

1922 - September - Scribner's follows with a second collection of Scott's short stories entitled *Tales of the Jazz Age*.

1924 - July - While in Europe together, Scott works on *The Great Gatsby*. Zelda courts the affections of a French aviator. Confronted by Scott, she ends her relationship with the dashing Frenchman.

1925 - April - *The Great Gatsby* is published by Scribner's to mixed reviews and disappointing sales.

1925 - May - Scott and Zelda meet Ernest Hemingway in Paris. Scott later recommends Hemingway to Maxwell Perkins at Scribner's.

1927 - Summer - At age twenty-seven, Zelda resumes ballet lessons, while also writing. Scott's output is diminished by his excessive drinking.

1930 - April - While in France, Zelda suffers her first mental breakdown. Diagnosed as a schizophrenic, she enters a clinic in Switzerland the next month. For the next year she remains in Switzerland, while Scott travels to France and the United States.

1930 - June - Upon the urging of their editor Maxwell Perkins, Tom Wolfe meets Scott at the Ritz Bar in Paris. Each had read the other's works, but Wolfe left unimpressed with Fitzgerald.

1930 - July - By coincidence, Tom and Scott happen upon each other in Switzerland, where Tom was working on his second novel.

1931 - September - Scott goes to Hollywood, where he works on scripts for M-G-M to earn money for Zelda's hospitalization, Scottie's private tuition, and his wasteful lifestyle.

1932 - February - Zelda enters Johns Hopkins University Hospital in Baltimore, where she writes the autobiographical *Save Me the Waltz*, while Scott struggles to finish his long overdue *Tender Is the Night*.

1932 - October - *Save Me the Waltz* sells just 1,392 copies. Zelda is crushed and their marriage is in shambles.

1934 - February - Zelda enters Sheppard-Pratt Hospital, a private psychiatric hospital in Towson, Maryland, after her third breakdown. Scott continues to live nearby, making regular trips to New York.

1934 - April - *Tender Is the Night* proves disappointing. Zelda's condition worsens, as she begins hallucinating. More frequently she has violent outbursts and talks openly about committing suicide.

1934 - June - Maxwell Perkins arranges a luncheon for Scott and Tom Wolfe, hoping they can persuade Wolfe to make revisions to his novel.

1935 - February 3 - Scott travels from Maryland to Tryon, North Carolina, taking 14-year-old Scottie out of private school. Nora and Lefty Flynn take Scottie into their home for the next three weeks while he writes.

1935- April - Scott believes he has tuberculosis, prompting him to make plans to journey to Asheville. Zelda, now convinced she is a messenger from God, remains at Sheppard-Pratt Hospital.

1935 - May 16 - Scott checks into the Grove Park Inn. He soon meets with Dr. Paul Ringer, who found Scott suffering from exhaustion, alcoholism, cirrhosis of the liver, and insomnia, but not tuberculosis.

1935 - June 12 - Scott travels back to Tryon to see his friends Nora and Lefty Flynn, who introduce him to best-selling author Margaret Culkin Banning, a divorced mother who eventually wrote thirty-six novels. Scott is jealous of Banning's financial success and shows no respect for her novels, many of which called for women's equality in the workforce.

1935 - June 18 - Scott initiates a disastrous affair with a married woman staying at the Grove Park Inn. The following week he travels back to Baltimore to visit Zelda for five days, then to New York City. He stays for a few days at the Oak Hall Hotel in Tryon working on a story.

1935- July 4 - Scott runs into Maxwell Perkins and Tom Wolfe in NYC.

1935 - July - Scott tries to rent a room from Julia Wolfe at the Old Kentucky Home, but is turned away when she sees he has been drinking.

1935 - July 19-21 - Scott stays at the Lake Lure Inn to avoid the husband of the married woman he is having an affair with at the Grove Park Inn.

1935 - July 24 - Scott goes to Baltimore to see Zelda for her birthday.

1935 - August - Scott checks into the Vanderbilt Hotel in Asheville under the name "Francis Key," as he meekly attempts to end the affair.

1935 - August 15 - Scott returns to the Grove Park Inn, checking into rooms 441 and 443. He begins drinking more heavily than ever. A local woman he begins sleeping with "found him to be fun and exciting, charming and lovable when sober, nasty and abusive when drunk."

1935 - September 13-19 - Scott checks himself into Mission Hospital in Asheville for exhaustion and the onset of pneumonia.

1935 - September 19 - Before leaving, Scott meets with Dr. Robert S. Carroll of Highland Hospital and plans to transfer Zelda in the spring.

1935 - Winter - Scott checks into the Skyland Hotel in Hendersonville, where he writes the three-part autobiographical series "The Crack-Up."

1936 - April 8 - Scott transfers Zelda to Highland Hospital for treatment for her nervous disorders. She continues to write and takes up painting. They drive down to Chimney Rock and Lake Lure that month.

1936 - July - On an outing with Zelda at the former Beaver Lake swimming pool, Scott dislocates his shoulder and breaks his collarbone, which requires a cumbersome cast for six weeks, during which time he attempts to dictate stories in his room at the Grove Park Inn.

1936 - September 25 - On the approach of his fortieth birthday Scott agrees to an interview with Michael Mok, a writer for the *New York Post*. The article entitled, "The Other Side of Paradise, Scott Fitzgerald, 40, Engulfed in Despair," was published the day after his birthday. Distraught, Scott attempts suicide by swallowing all of what remained of his pain pills, but vomits on the bathroom floor of his hotel room.

1937 - January thru July - Scott returns to the Oak Hall Hotel in Tryon.

1937 - May 5 - Tom Wolfe visits Scott at the Oak Hall Hotel.

1937 - July - Scott signs a six-month contract with M-G-M in Hollywood for $1,000 a week. He is assigned various writing projects, all of which frustrate Scott, who in turn irritates his co-writers and producers.

1937 - July - Scott meets movie reviewer and celebrity gossip columnist Sheila Graham in Hollywood. He soon moves into her apartment.

1938 - December - M-G-M refuses to renew Scott's contract.

1939 - Scott starts his final novel, *The Last Tycoon.*

1939 - December - Zelda travels to Montgomery to visit her mother.

1940 - April - Zelda, now forty years old, is released after four years of hospitalization in Asheville into the care of her mother.

1940 - December 21 - Scott suffers a fatal heart attack in Sheila Graham's apartment. He is buried a week later at the Rockville Union Cemetery in Maryland. Twenty-five people attend the service.

1941 - October - Scribner's publishes *The Last Tycoon.*

1943 - February - Scottie is married in New York, but Zelda is not able to attend. "In my next incarnation," Scottie later wrote, "I may not choose again to be the daughter of a Famous Author. The pay is good and there are fringe benefits, but the working conditions are too hazardous. I knew there was only one way for me to survive my parents' tragedy, and that was to ignore it."

1943 - August - Zelda checks herself into Asheville's Highland Hospital for a seven-month recuperation. She writes to a friend, "Asheville is haunted by unhappy, uncharted remembrance for me."

1943 - September 6 - Zelda decides to move over to the Old Kentucky Home, where Julia Wolfe assigns her "a room with two windows for $3.50 a week." It is unclear how long she stayed.

1944 - February - Zelda returns to her family home in Montgomery, where she again becomes intensely religious.

1947 - November 2 - Zelda comes back to Highland Hospital for a series of insulin treatments for her anxiety. She is assigned a room on the top floor while she recuperates.

1948 - March 10 - That night a fire breaks out in the hospital's basement kitchen, quickly spreading up a dumbwaiter shaft in the old wooden structure, trapping Zelda and others on the top floor. While the staff was able to get most of the women out of the lower floors, nine women, including Zelda, perish in the flames.

1948 - March 17 - Zelda is buried beside Scott.

1975 - November 7 - Upon Scottie's request, Scott and Zelda are reburied without fanfare in the Fitzgerald family plot at St. Mary's Catholic Church Cemetery in Rockville, Maryland.

"I wouldn't mind a bit if in a few years Zelda and I could snuggle up together under a stone in some old graveyard here. That is really a happy thought and not melancholy at all." – Scott Fitzgerald, 1935

Asheville: A Timeline

Four hundred and eighty million years ago, a massive struggle silently raging beneath the earth's surface came to a grinding halt, leaving in its wake the ancient Appalachian Mountains. Once as tall and as rugged as the youthful Rocky Mountains, erosion eventually softened the sharp mountain peaks, permitting vast stands of oak, pine, and chestnut forests to flourish on its slopes. Within an area called the Blue Ridge Mountains lay a lush, fertile plateau, forty miles wide by sixty miles long. With an average elevation of 2,200 feet and nourished by the French Broad River, the mountaintop plateau served as home to centuries of native tribes, including Paleo, Archaic, Woodland, Iroquois, and Cherokee Indians, who fished, hunted, and fought to protect their territory from other tribes and the white settlers who later discovered their beautiful valley.

1540 – Spanish explorers under the command of Hernando de Soto entered the region in search of gold. They introduced the Cherokee to guns, horses, and smallpox. De Soto later died on the expedition. To prevent the Indians from unearthing him, his men dropped his weighted body into the Mississippi River. Over the course of the next two centuries, colorful descriptions of the Appalachian Mountains attracted a growing number of trappers, traders, and settlers, leading to deadly encounters with many of the Cherokee tribes.

1776 – After reports of the murder of white settlers by Cherokee Indians, General Griffith Rutherford was sent into western North Carolina to destroy as many Indian villages as he could find, effectively securing the area around what would become Asheville.

1789 – The colony of North Carolina officially became a state of the Union. As a result, the federal government accelerated its free land grant program as a reward for Revolutionary War soldiers and to further encourage development of the western region.

1792 – The area around Asheville was formally named Buncombe County in honor of Revolutionary War hero Colonel Edward Buncombe, even though Colonel Buncombe had never been to Buncombe County. Local officials hoped that naming their county after a wealthy eastern plantation owner would please influential state politicians in Raleigh. Colonel Buncombe fought bravely in the war and is often reported to have died while being held captive by the British. In truth, after being severely wounded and captured at Germantown in 1777, Colonel Buncombe was released by the British. A short time later, he fell down the stairs where he was staying in Philadelphia, broke open his wounds, and bled to death.

Nearly fifty years later, during a congressional filibuster, a representative from Asheville stood at the podium, stalling for time, declaring, "I am only speaking for Buncombe." The phrase caught on and soon the word Buncombe, often shortened to 'bunkum,' also came to mean 'nonsense' or 'foolish talk.'

1795 – The small settlement of Morristown, located at an important crossroads above the banks of the French Broad River, was renamed Asheville in honor of Governor Samuel Ashe. Incorporated in 1797, Asheville was officially recognized as the county seat by the state's general assembly.

1828 – The completion of the Buncombe Turnpike, running from Greeneville, Tennessee to Greenville, South Carolina and passing directly through what is now Pack Square in downtown Asheville, insured the continued growth of the village. At that time, it was home to an estimated 350 people. More than 200,000 hogs were driven along the turnpike each year, along with cattle, sheep, and turkeys. Teams of horses pulling wagons piled with goods, as well as stagecoaches filled with curious tourists and hardy settlers, passed through Asheville. Although some sections several miles south of Asheville were actually covered with rough-hewn planks, most of the wide turnpike consisted of packed dirt and gravel. The raw wood planks tended to warp, loosen, and buckle under the sun and rain, actually impeding travel by wagon or stagecoach, so the practice was soon discontinued.

Once the railroad reached Asheville in 1880, the Buncombe Turnpike gradually fell to the wayside. Some sections eventually became 20th century automobile roads; traces of others can still be found in woods and fields south of Asheville, where they are traversed by hikers and horseback riders, often unaware of the history beneath their feet.

1861 – By the outbreak of the Civil War, the population of Asheville had increased to 1,100. Unlike their Southern neighbors, Buncombe County farmers and Asheville residents had never grown dependent upon slavery as a keystone to their rural economy. While reluctant to take up arms to defend the plantation system, they were willing to fight for their state's rights against what they saw as the growing intrusion of the federal government into their lives. In 1861, North Carolina voted to secede from the Union. In Asheville, canons were placed strategically atop the encircling mountains to defend the city against an anticipated Union attack. Hundreds of its young men enlisted in the Confederate army, serving with distinction at the battles of Gettysburg, Chickamauga, Bethel, and Appomattox. Back home, Asheville served primarily as a distribution, training, and reconnaissance center for the Confederacy, with a small but respected rifle factory, an armory, and a military hospital on the town square.

1865 – Asheville's only skirmish occurred on April 6, just three days before General Lee's final surrender, when a Union scouting party approached Asheville from the north. Alerted by a black servant who had raced ahead of the Union soldiers, a hastily assembled band of Asheville volunteers repelled the invaders, firing from elevated earthen works dug in the vicinity of today's University of North Carolina campus. The only fatality was a Union soldier who fell off his horse into the French Broad River and drowned. The battle effectively ended after five hours of sporadic rifle fire when darkness and a heavy thunderstorm sent both sides scurrying for cover. In their hasty retreat the Union soldiers left behind several rifles, canteens, and pieces of equipment, plus "a man's leg, clad in blue, still in a boot," an apparent casualty of the rebel canon fire.

1876 – The publication of a popular novel entitled *Land of the Sky*, with glowing descriptions of Buncombe County and Asheville, increased pressure on the railroads to find a way over, around, and through the multiple tiers of steep mountains encircling the town. Surveyors and engineers devised winding switchbacks, towering wooden bridges, and deep tunnels, only to see their plans delayed by legislative squabbling in Raleigh. In addition, deadly landslides and cave-ins cost the lives of more than two hundred men digging tunnels, cutting ledges, and laying rails. Most of the men killed during construction were black convicts sent by the North Carolina legislature from eastern prisons. Many were unable to escape rock slides and cave-ins because of the padlocked chains and iron shackles around their ankles. The dead were buried by other convicts near wherever they fell.

1880 – On October 2 the first steam locomotive emerged from the steep mountain peaks east of Asheville, powering its way past the villages of Old Fort and Black Mountain. It came to a halt at the city's first railway station in what is now Biltmore Village, setting off a city-wide celebration

163.

by the 2,500 residents. In the rush to open the final tunnel near Swannanoa, the foremen failed to adequately fortify the dirt walls. While the people in Asheville were celebrating, a final cave-in at the west opening of the tunnel crushed twenty-one men to death.

Within weeks Asheville was swelling with curious tourists, eventually including wealthy entrepreneurs with names now familiar to Asheville residents and visitors, including George Pack, Edwin Wiley Grove, Frank Coxe, and George Vanderbilt. In addition to building mansions for their families, men such as these also saw the opportunity to construct hotels and office buildings, start residential developments, found businesses, and fund libraries, hospitals, parks, and schools.

1885 – Riverside Cemetery was established by the city; earlier burials in small churchyards along Church Street were moved to the new cemetery.

1895 – George Vanderbilt moved into his 250-room Biltmore House designed by architect Richard Morris Hunt. The master plan for the 125,000-acre grounds was created by Frederick Law Olmsted. After Vanderbilt's unexpected death from complications after an appendectomy in 1914, his widow sold approximately 87,000 acres to the United States government to become part of the Pisgah National Forest. Additional land was later sold for residential developments, reducing the acreage around the mansion to approximately 8,000 acres today.

1897 – The area's first professional baseball team was named the Asheville Moonshiners. In 1915 the name was changed to the Asheville Tourists. In 1923 the team moved into McCormick Field, which stood until 1992, when it was torn down and rebuilt on the same site.

1900 – On October 3, Thomas Clayton Wolfe was born in the family home at 92 Woodfin Street. It was the area's reputation as a health resort that in 1880 had brought to Asheville stone cutter William Oliver Wolfe and his second wife Cynthia, who died of tuberculosis in 1884. Wolfe then married Julia Westall, descended from an established Asheville family, and together they raised seven children, Tom being the youngest.

1906 – Julia Wolfe purchased a downtown boarding house called the Old Kentucky Home. Her reluctance to turn away any cash boarder, even those exhibiting the symptoms of tuberculosis, is believed to have contributed to the deaths of two of her sons, Benjamin and Tom.

Convinced the town should be developed into a health resort, around this time a number of local officials began a national advertising campaign, touting its clean mountain air, tranquil scenery, and quality food at such heralded hotels as the stately 1886 Battery Park Hotel, a rambling Queen Anne hotel atop twenty-two acres of flower gardens and manicured lawns overlooking downtown Asheville. The campaign attracted a number of prominent physicians working to find a cure for tuberculosis, as well as influential businessmen in need of a place to rest and recuperate, including Edwin Wiley Grove and George Vanderbilt.

Unfortunately, the campaign also spawned a large number of unregulated boarding houses which catered to victims of highly contagious tuberculosis. Alarmed at the growing number of invalids walking the streets of Asheville, another group of citizens and city officials began warning the population that these unsavory boarding houses would reverse the city's growing reputation as a safe, desirable resort destination. As a result, city and county officials gradually closed the more deplorable boarding houses, while also rejecting a proposal for a national tuberculosis center, paving the way for Asheville to continue to safely attract visitors and new residents from across the country.

1907 – Thirteen years before national prohibition, the people of Asheville voted to outlaw the manufacture and sale of liquor. At the time Asheville had fifteen restaurants and sixteen saloons. The law did not prohibit personal possession of liquor or its consumption, only the manufacture or sale of it within city limits, making the statute difficult for law officers to enforce. Prohibition was repealed nationwide in 1933.

1913 – On July 12 Edwin Wiley Grove hosted an inaugural banquet for four hundred male guests at the 150-room Grove Park Inn, designed and constructed on the western slope of Sunset Mountain by his son-in-law Frederick Loring Seely. Secretary of State William Jennings Bryan was the guest of honor. Bryan later constructed a home on Kimberly Avenue designed by architect Richard Sharpe Smith.

1916 – On Sunday, July 16, after two consecutive hurricanes each stalled over the Blue Ridge Mountains, triggering nearly two weeks of torrential downpours, swelling streams, saturating hillsides, and spilling over dams, the waters of both the French Broad and the Swannanoa Rivers came barreling down upon Asheville. More than a mile wide and armed with entire trees, bridge timbers, farm equipment, buildings, and automobiles, the rising tide of turbulent water battered and destroyed everything in its path, from railroad bridges to hundreds of structures, causing millions of dollars in damages and killing eighty people over the course of three deadly days.

1918 – The November 11 armistice which ended World War I signaled the beginning of a great boom for Asheville, as scores of buildings were razed to make way for more than sixty larger, taller modern structures. The downtown district expanded from Pack Square west along Patton Avenue and College Street, as well as north along Haywood Street, Lexington Avenue, and Broadway.

1922 – Edwin Wiley Grove razed the 1886 Battery Park Hotel, replacing it in 1924 with a fourteen-story brick hotel by the same name. Five years later, the 77-year-old Grove died in his top floor penthouse suite.

1923 – Developer L.B. Jackson tore down the former W.O. Wolfe tombstone shop, making way for the fifteen-story, Jackson Building also completed in 1924. Near the end of the boom, architect Douglas Ellington designed four notable Art Deco buildings: the First Baptist Church (1927), the City Building (1928), the S&W Cafeteria (1929), and the Asheville High School (1929). At that time the population of Asheville surpassed 30,000, while attracting an estimated 250,000 visitors each year.

1929 – Two weeks after the release of Thomas Wolfe's scandalous novel *Look Homeward, Angel,* the stock market crash brought the country and Asheville to its knees. When the Central Bank and Trust Company failed in 1930, the city of Asheville lost or owed over forty million dollars. Distraught over his failure to better protect the city's bank deposits, on February 25, 1930, Mayor Gallatin Roberts ended his life in a fourth-floor bathroom in the downtown Legal Building. His final letter ended, "I have given my life for my city, and I am innocent. I did what I thought was right." A later investigation cleared Roberts of any crimes.

1930 – Upon the request of city officials, Edith Vanderbilt agreed to open the Biltmore House and grounds to the public to encourage tourism for Asheville. The population of the city climbed past 50,000 residents. The Beaucatcher Mountain Tunnel was also completed, providing easy access between homes and businesses on either side of the mountain. The highly controversial "Beaucatcher Cut" adjacent to the tunnel was blasted out for Interstate 240 in 1980.

1935 – Convinced he had contracted tuberculosis, author F. Scott Fitzgerald arrived at the Grove Park Inn on May 16 and remained in the area for much of the next two years. He also stayed at the Skyland Hotel in Hendersonville, the George Vanderbilt Hotel and the Battery Park Hotel in downtown Asheville, the Oak Hall Hotel in Tryon, and the Lake Lure

Inn. His biographers and medical experts doubt Fitzgerald ever had tuberculosis, but did suffer from exhaustion, anxiety, and alcoholism.

1938 – Once scorned by the same Asheville people, the town turned out to see Thomas Wolfe laid to rest after his death on September 15 at age thirty-eight. People stood outside the packed First Presbyterian Church during his funeral and lined the city streets to view his hearse making its way to Riverside Cemetery.

1948 – A kitchen fire on the night of March 10 in the lower level of Highland Hospital swept up the shaft of a dumbwaiter and raced down the hallways of the wooden structure, killing nine women who had been sleeping in rooms with bars on the windows. Among them was Zelda Fitzgerald. Her remains were discovered amid the charred rubble beside one of her red ballerina slippers. Her identity was confirmed by her dental records. She was buried in Rockville, MD, beside Scott, who had died of a heart attack on December 21, 1940 at the age of forty-four. Zelda was just forty-eight.

1949 – Four years after Julia Wolfe's death, her boarding house was restored and reopened as the Thomas Wolfe Memorial. In 1974 the boarding house was deeded to the state of North Carolina. One year after the Visitor Center opened in 1997, an arsonist set fire to the house. After a six-year restoration, it was reopened in 2004.

1955 – Charles Sammons, a Dallas billionaire, bought the Grove Park Inn and undertook an extensive renovation and expansion program that continued beyond his death in 1988; it was then led by the efforts of his wife Elaine, who passed away in 2009. Omni Hotels and Resorts purchased the iconic Asheville landmark in 2013.

1979 – The first Bele Chere street festival was held in July to draw tourists and residents to downtown Asheville. It grew to become the largest outdoor festival in the Southeast, annually attracting more than 350,000 attendees. An eventual victim of its own success, the final festival was held in 2013 after complaints from downtown business owners that the festival, which cost taxpayers more than $200,000 to host, was actually hurting their business.

1990s – Asheville continued to grow, as its population surpassed 60,000 residents. Mission Memorial Hospital merged with St. Joseph's Hospital; the two daily newspapers became one morning publication; a new

McCormick Field was constructed for the minor league baseball team; historic structures, such as the Manor Inn, the Grove Arcade, and the S&W Cafeteria, were saved and restored; both the Grove Park Inn and the Biltmore Estate undertook extensive expansion programs; and a new and expanded Visitor Center opened at the Thomas Wolfe Memorial.

Into the 21st Century – The unique combination of the serene Blue Ridge Mountains, a treasure trove of architectural landmarks, a lively down-town music, arts, and shopping scene, a fascinating history, numerous cozy neighborhoods, and popular outdoor events, adventures, and activities – all set in a year-round moderate climate – has propelled Asheville onto scores of Top Ten lists of places to live, enjoy, invest, visit, and retire. Its population has surpassed 90,000 residents and Buncombe county attracts more than 11 million visitors each year. The building boom which began in 2001 shows no sign of slowing, as developers continue to build condominiums, apartments, commercial buildings, and residential neighborhoods, creating yet a future chapter to be added to Asheville's unique and fascinating history.

Biltmore House under construction, c. 1893.
(North Carolina Collection, Pack Memorial Library, Asheville, NC.)

Index

Recommended Reading

After the Good Gay Times: 1935, A Season with F. Scott Fitzgerald by Tony Buttitta, Viking Press, 1974.

Asheville's Historic Architecture by Richard Hansley, Arcadia, 2011.

Asheville's Riverside Cemetery by Joshua Darty, Arcadia, 2011.

Thomas Wolfe by Andrew Turnbull, Charles Scribner's Sons, 1967.

Max Perkins: Editor of Genius by A. Scott Berg, 1978.

Look Homeward: A Life of Thomas Wolfe by David Herbert Donald, Little, Brown, 1987.

Thomas Wolfe: A Writer's Life by Ted Mitchell, 1997.

The Sons of Maxwell Perkins: The Letters of F. Scott Fitzgerald, Ernest Hemingway, Thomas Wolfe, and Their Editor edited by Matthew J. Bruccoli, University of South Carolina Press, 2004.

Thomas Wolfe: An Illustrated Biography by Ted Mitchell, 2006.

I'd Die For You, And Other Lost Stories edited by Anne Margaret Daniel, Scribner Publishing, 2017.

Some Sort of Epic Grandeur: The Life of F. Scott Fitzgerald by Matthew Bruccoli, University of South Carolina Press, 2002.

Dear Scott, Dearest Zelda: The Love Letters of F. Scott and Zelda Fitzgerald edited by Jackson Bryer, St. Martin's Press, 2002.

Zelda: A Biography by Nancy Milford, Harper & Row, 1970.

Scott Fitzgerald by Andrew Turnbull, Charles Scribner's Sons, 1962.

The Letters of F. Scott Fitzgerald edited by Andrew Turnbull, 1963.

For a list of books written by Thomas Wolfe, Zelda Sayre Fitzgerald, and F. Scott Fitzgerald, please see their timelines on pages 151-160.

About the Author

Bruce Johnson moved to Asheville in 1988, the same year he founded the National Arts and Crafts Conference held each February at the 1913 Grove Park Inn. He has since written several books on the Grove Park Inn and the Arts and Crafts movement, receiving a Griffin Award, the *Als ik Kan* Award, and the Thomas Wolfe Memorial Literary Award. He is currently working on a book on Biltmore Industries and its founders Eleanor Vance and Charlotte Yale. He and his wife Leigh Ann Hamon live on a small farm outside Asheville. For more information, please go to: BruceJohnsonBooks.com.